MEETING MANAGEMENT:

A PROFESSIONAL APPROACH

MEETING MANAGEMENT

A PROFESSIONAL APPROACH

James E. Jones

Edited by Connie Schott

BAYARD PUBLICATIONS   **STAMFORD, CONNECTICUT**

Bayard Publications, Inc.
695 Summer Street
Stamford, Connecticut 06901

Copyright © 1979 by Bayard Publications, Inc.

Library of Congress Catalog Card Number: 78-74192
ISBN: 0-933266-00-9

FIRST EDITION
Printed in the United States of America by the Science Press
Design by C. Edward Cerullo
Typography by New Canaan Graphic Arts

Dedication

This book is for meeting planners, would-be meeting planners, and the fine hotel and other service personnel who assist them in their professional activities.

CONTENTS

APPENDIX

PREFACE

When I began my career in meeting management there was little information on the subject available. There were, however, a couple of fine people who were currently planning meetings for other companies, and they helped me immeasureably by sharing with me the hard lessons they had learned through experience.

I went on to develop—in the course of a great deal of trial and error training—my own system of professional meeting management. I have written this book because I want to share it with you. I have written it because I believe that by sharing my experience with the important people who now function, or who will function, as meeting planners and as members of the hospitality service industry I can help them to do a better, easier—more *professional*—job. I believe that by so doing I can help not only to promote more successful meetings but to take us one step further in bringing the vitally important field of meeting planning—and the bright, courageous men and women who function as meeting planners—the recognition it and they deserve in the realm of corporate and association activity.

James E. Jones

Part One

**BEHIND THE MEETING:
CONCEPTS AND PHILOSOPHY**

I

PERSPECTIVE
ON
MEETING MANAGEMENT

I have often been asked: Why is there a need for professional meeting management? How do you look upon the job of the professional meeting manager? How would you define it? My answer:

> **The primary job of the professional meeting manager is to permit other professionals within his or her organization to devote 100% of their time to what they do best—their jobs!**

The planner who accomplishes this is contributing in a major, substantial way to the success of an organization or business by providing a service which permits other people to *maximize the value of their time.*

Time is man's most precious possession! But while it is commonly accepted that an organization's most valuable assets are its people and the *time* they devote to accomplishing its objectives and goals, many corporations and associations tend to treat their executives' time as if it were both inexhaustible and inexpensive.

Such organizations would do well to realize that when they allow employees to run helter skelter in all directions they are not only performing inefficiently but are probably neither as profitable nor as effective as they might be.

MEETINGS ARE AN INVESTMENT

Companies and associations conduct meetings for a variety of reasons. They use them to inform and educate their representatives. They use them to motivate them to attain higher goals—and to reward them and inspire them to even greater success when those goals have been reached. A meeting can be a training seminar, an executive conference—or a full-fledged convention . . .

But whatever the reason or the occasion of the meeting, it is a two-pronged investment. On the one hand is the direct dollar cost—for items such as transportation, room and board, meeting room charges, speakers. On the other is the indirect cost—of people time.

Direct vs. Indirect Cost

The traditional concept of meeting management evaluates a meeting on the basis of direct, tangible dollar expenditure alone. The reason for this is that direct dollar costs for all visible aspects of the meeting—such as room and board and transportation—are easy to calculate. Simple accounts show clear evidence of the expenses involved.

Direct dollar expenditure, however, is only one part of the meeting investment. *Indirect dollar expenses* often far outweigh direct dollar costs. The most hidden cost is probably that on the part of the delegate who takes time away from his regular business, spends it preparing for the meeting and faces an adjustment when he returns. The dollar value of the time spent outside of one's normal pursuits is tremendous!

A more obvious indirect cost would be that of an executive

participating in a business program who spends hours of preparation for a twenty or thirty minute formal presentation. He may also require support from his art department and audio-visual department in order to make his presentation meaningful—more people time! The speech may be part of his job but, nevertheless, the price is great in view of alternative business uses of his time.

To measure meeting investment more accurately, it is necessary to consider both the *direct* and *indirect* cost. The investment of people time—when a price tag is placed upon it—will prove staggering. Using a concept of meeting investment analysis which combines direct *and* indirect cost not only places proper levels of responsibility on meeting management, but puts the true cost of the business program in proper perspective. Applying the number of hours spent in formal business sessions during a meeting equates to an hourly unit cost often ranging from $5,000 to $100,000. And given that enormous price, the business program participant soon realizes the need for a performance which is equal to the investment.

CENTRALIZED MEETING PLANNING

In many companies and associations the meeting planning function has been rotated annually, a practice which in itself creates a part-timer syndrome of perpetual mediocrity. In addition, many executives tend to look upon hotel selection and meeting site coordination as a rather enjoyable sojourn from their regular work routine. They are reluctant to give it up even though the errors they make are costly and generate unprofitable meetings. This practice is allowed to continue simply because the organization does not have the measurement skills to evaluate this lack of effectiveness.

Successful meetings are pure luck in such organizations. The lessons of the past are never applied effectively to the future unless there is a well-defined vehicle for continuity. Effective meeting analysis, however, disallows such a hit-or-miss approach to meeting management.

All organizations that conduct meetings regularly should review what they are doing and give serious consideration to centralizing meeting planning functions. If they conduct only a few meetings so that this does not seem feasible, they should consider hiring an outside firm to handle meeting planning.

In some smaller organizations centralization of meeting planning may require one individual to devote a major percentage of his or her time to meeting management, leaving the remainder of the working time for some other part of the business. In larger organizations, however, a full-time person with a separate department may be required to perform the meeting planning operation. This, of course, depends upon the frequency and size of meetings and the needs of the organization.

By centralizing responsibility the organization not only provides a vehicle for learning effectively from experience but also clearly identifies the individual who is in charge of all facets of meeting management. And at any rate, in today's environment of intense competition and high costs, corporate and association executives must question the quality of the leadership they are providing if they do not supply professional meeting services for their people.

THE ROLE OF THE MEETING MANAGER

Often a company has neither a centralized meeting planning department nor a clear perspective of the role of the meeting planner. Such a person is viewed as being responsible merely for last minute details and coordination. If, however, the organization can accept the premise that meetings are an investment—in dollars as well as people time—then it will realize that in this context the meeting planner is a financial manager, an investment counselor.

Implementation of the financial manager concept is of vital importance to the economic well-being of the organization. And chances are that the organization that recognizes and appreciates the value of professional meeting management—with responsibility for maximizing the investment of time and money—is a progressive, profitable operation.

Evaluation Of Meeting Management Talent

When a company or association has an unclear perspective of the role of the meeting planner, the job is usually performed by a person whose ability is limited to simple detail coordination. The result is meetings that reflect the talent put to work on the planning—low quality.

Another frequent mistake is to evaluate a professional meeting planner in terms of his or her impact on direct costs alone. Any properly trained professional planner can justify the cost of time and services by direct savings on rates, gratuities and other factors which his or her knowledge and experience encompass. The major contribution of the professional meeting planner, however, is the impact of his or her function on the utilization of fellow executives' time.

Who Is A Meeting Planner?

Running a successful meeting is hard work, physically and mentally. The effective professional meeting manager is, therefore, sound of mind and body. He or she has to be even-tempered under pressure, intelligent and extremely well organized in order to meet the demands of a grueling, often intense, job.

A professional meeting planner is a leader, a negotiator and a diplomat who works equally well alone and as a member of a team. He or she is flexible enough to cope with ever-changing situations on the spot, but sufficiently purposeful to be able to keep everything in the proper perspective.

The professional meeting manager is, first and foremost, a people person—outgoing, versatile and possessed of excellent communicative skills. He or she has learned from experience that the challenge of managing interpersonal relationships is always compounded by the fact that it must be accomplished in a strange physical environment.

Communicative skills—verbal, written and interpersonal—are necessary to motivate hotels and service organizations to do the best possible job for the meeting at hand. And at the same time, the planner must effectively deal with his group—a conglomeration of personalities and egos exhibiting various degrees of vanity, pride, selfishness and hypersensitivity.

The professional meeting planner knows what the job entails—in every detail. He or she takes everything, including criticism, in stride, applies it to the job and is continually learning and growing. The professional's goal is always to do the job better, to make meetings more effective, more meaningful—a good investment for the company or association.

Training, Experience And Acceptance

Even though many companies are now aware of the value of such professional meeting management, there has been until recently only a limited supply of competent talent available. A major reason is the lack of education and training. Colleges, companies and associations have been unable to provide an educational program to train meeting managers properly. And without a definitive training program, people who find themselves gravitating toward a career in meeting management have had to band together to educate themselves by sharing ideas and experiences and developing their own concepts. All of this is educational and helpful, but it is my firm belief that the basic principles and techniques of meeting planning can be taught. These generic concepts are the same from company to company, association to association—and even country to country.

Effective meeting management in today's world is a necessity which no would-be profitable and prestigious enterprise can afford to overlook. And the professional meeting planner—the individual investment expert who accepts the responsibility for planning all facets of conferences, conventions and seminars—deserves recognition as the important and influential executive he or she is.

II

THE PLIGHT OF THE MEETING PLANNER

Good meeting planning is often taken for granted. When all goes well, people forget to take into account the countless hours spent, the specialized knowledge required—and the intimate concern for every little detail that the planner has provided. If all does not go well, however, the planner is the first to be criticized.

Particularly irritating is the viewpoint of other members of the organization that the planner's job is a glamorous one of constant travel to new and exciting places and therefore an easy one. "So you're off on another trip," they say. "Working hard in Palm Springs, are you?" "Boy, if only I had a job like yours!" Such remarks demonstrate an obvious lack of understanding of what it takes to plan, conduct and supervise a successful meeting.

But how are they to know and understand what goes into planning a meeting when there are no widely circulated and accepted concepts and definitions? The answer is to develop an acceptable, recognizable job description. But when there are over 75,000 meeting planners in the country, doing so is indeed a formidable task.

Why The Problem?

Formal education in meeting management has been slow in developing, the reason being that there have been too few students interested in meeting management as a career. Schools like Cornell, the University of Michigan and Metropolitan State College in Denver are making attempts, but until recently many students have been unable to obtain a degree in meeting management simply because it does not exist in most curricula.

There is also a noticeable lack of good written material on meeting management. Several books on the "nuts and bolts," the how-to's of specific aspects of meeting management have appeared, but the field has very little conceptual writing to form a basis for meaningful and uniform national job descriptions, performance standards and management evaluations. Meeting planners who have shown progress in establishing proper status, credibility and support have done so as a result of individual effort without benefit of professional standards of performance.

The typical meeting planner is a part-timer with various other duties besides meeting planning. National profiles, in fact, indicate that the typical planner conducts only four to seven meetings per year. It should be noted, however, that you do not have to do the job full time in order to be a professional. Professionalism is not exclusive of part-time.

Another problem is that in all but large companies and associations, the responsibility for planning meetings is splintered without a centralized planning service for even the most crucial meetings. A few industries, such as the insurance industry, have experienced significant growth in centralized meeting management, but such growth has generally reflected the strength of unique people within an organization rather than a conscious, well-thought-out plan of action by the employing organization.

There is another problem concurrent with the difficulties of a part-timer doing numerous jobs for an organization without a centralized meeting planning operation. That is that there is at most a very small group—usually a group of one—in any given company doing meeting planning. That job, therefore, cannot generally be taught in-house; in most cases you cannot "train" for the job in an assistant capacity as you can for many other positions.

If the meeting planner has made one consistent error over the years it is that . . .

Too little time has been spent educating superiors and other key executives as to what is involved in planning and conducting a successful meeting.

Meeting planning organizations have compounded this error by failing to devote any time or money to educating employing organizations as to the value of the services rendered by the meeting planner.

The emergence of good leadership in the meeting planning field has been slow. Many young people have been attracted to the field, but have subsequently left due to the lack of a clear career path and of appropriate recognition and compensation programs. The situation has significantly improved in recent years; and today we have many talented young men and women just waiting to assume the reins of leadership. It is the responsibility of seasoned meeting planners to provide them with the tools to finish the job which has been started.

ESTABLISHING CREDIBILITY

Action a meeting planner can take to build recognition and support within an organization will include the following:

Adopt A Positive Attitude

Face each day with a positive attitude. It is not productive to talk about "blame" or "fault" for the current situation; and the largest share of responsibility for changing it must rest with meeting planners since they will benefit most from the change. A firm belief in oneself and the value of professional meeting services is essential to accomplishing this desirable objective.

Be Assertive

Through study of professional meeting management techniques and of the industry in which one works, planners must become more knowledgeable—and thus prepared to be more assertive. Too many planners strive too hard to please and to be liked—rather than respected—by other members of their organization. A more assertive role—one in which you are willing to sell yourself and your ideas to others—will correct this. A change in basic social and business styles is not necessary, but you must be willing to take a strong position whenever basic principles of good meeting management are violated by the organization.

Expand The Concept Of The Job

Although the planner may not be responsible for the total business program of a meeting, he or she can at all times contribute to the success of the program by sharing ideas and knowledge. Basic educational techniques can be applied to all meetings, regardless of content; and it is the planner's responsibility to *learn* and *share* these techniques. One very important concept in this regard is that of the *value of executive time.* Share it with your organization as it clearly illustrates the need for meeting planning services and affords a meaningful measuring stick for the evaluation of the job's success.

Distinguish Between "Personal Power" And "Positional Power"

Positional power is easy to recognize. Doctors have it. Military officers have it. Major corporate officers have it. Positional power is what others say we are. It is exemplified by the uniform, by the name on the door and by the stationery or business card.

Personal power is not so easy to recognize. It is who you are all the time—the power of self-respect. We all take into every relationship the power that comes from feeling good about ourselves, liking ourselves and believing that the service we render is meaningful and important. The key to personal power, then, is knowledge and the full development of yourself as a person.

Personal power, as it relates to meeting planning, means that through hard work, self-study and a "serve-first" philosophy, you feel good about yourself—confident of your knowledge and of your ability to contribute positively to successful meetings. You like and accept the job you perform. You recognize who you are and respect yourself as a professional. You want to be liked, but you will never abdicate your own self-respect. Rather, you want to be respected for your contributions. And you should not be intimidated by positional power. Respect it; but never be subservient to it!

The person who operates from positional power ("Do it because I said so!") gets, at best, resentful compliance. But the person who can take into a relationship a unique brand of personal power can earn commitment from others.

Meeting planners must strive, through education and performance, to develop a brand of personal power that makes people want to promote and assist them in their growth within the organization. The meeting planner moving up the ladder should bear in mind that the ultimate goal is positional power matched by personal power. When the two are in harmony, success is assured.

Believe In The Investment Concept

Meetings are an investment of money as well as time—the time of the people who attend the meeting. As a person striving to maximize the return on a major investment, then, the meeting planner is a financial manager.

Implement A Customer-Client Relationship

If you work for a large organization or corporation, you service many different groups and departments in your meeting planning operation. In one day you may consult with the president of the company as well as the newest staff trainer and a whole battery of public relations and advertising people. But regardless of the status or job of each person you work with, that person should be looked upon as a vital customer and client. Take every opportunity to teach each person what you do and why, for you are seeking to earn the trust and respect of the people you service.

You want your clients to know that putting together a meeting is a complex task. Give them copies of the correspondence relating to their meeting; invite them to attend an advance review session with the hotel staff; let them observe the large number of people it will take to make their particular meeting a success. Under special circumstances you might furnish the client with a copy of the hotel's specificaton sheets for the meeting. These are often impressive documents listing the myriad details that must be juggled to manage a meeting successfully. Go out of your way to introduce clients to suppliers of meeting services—airline personnel, hotel staff, audio-visual staff, photographers.

Be sure you are the one to initiate, direct and control client involvement in the running of a meeting. This is the best way to educate them as to *what you do* and *why*. Successful performance of the complexities of your job—combined with understanding and appreciation on the part of clients—will be the prime source of strength in assuring proper organizational credibility, recognition and support for your planning activities.

Establish A Good Relationship With Your Boss

The planner's relationship with his or her immediate superior should be an open one based on continual education and communication. You cannot assume that your boss understands either you or your job, so take every opportunity to inform your boss about the growing complexity of your job. After all, with a heavy travel schedule you are frequently out of the office and it is only common courtesy to keep the boss informed as to where you are, why and for how long.

Invite the boss to accompany you on a complex inspection and planning visit in order to experience living out of a suitcase, jet lag, working with strangers, lonely hotel rooms, people late for appointments, ill-prepared suppliers of services and all the unexpected crises that necessitate another day or two on the road.

Have the boss accompany you and work your schedule when you are on-site, supervising a major meeting. A firsthand view of the multitude of people you must deal with and the unique management and communication skills you must exercise to do your job will be worth more than a thousand words on this subject.

You can also clip and forward to your boss meaningful articles on meeting management. Work hard at educating your boss because it is important to you that this executive be your biggest booster and supporter.

Share Problems

When major problems arise that are outside your personal control (bad weather, delayed flights, insufficient rooms, a guest speaker who gets sick, a major last-minute program change, a medical emergency) do not assume that your boss or your client has any understanding or appreciation of what you must do or go through to make the best of the situation. Solve the problems to the best of your ability, but make sure you use such situations to demonstrate your on-the-spot, under-pressure problem-solving expertise. Problems and their solutions often better illustrate the value of your services as a professional meeting planner than a smooth running meeting of great complexity. Make negatives positives through the appropriate involvement of others.

Learn What Goes Into The Evaluation Of High-Level Jobs In Your Organization

Consult with your boss or personnel officer to learn what techniques are used in higher level job evaluations. Determine which factors are evaluated in comparing one job to another. Job complexity and creativity are often highly rated, as are foresight, imagination, analytical ability, ingenuity and good judgment.

A job's scope and impact are also considered in evaluations. The importance of the work assigned in a job is measured, as well as its impact on the growth of the company—new business, customer relations, finances, operating expenses and human resources.

Often very specialized knowledge and skills are required to do a job properly. And of course, persuasive and managerial skills are always evaluated highly.

Your company or association must have some standards for evaluating the meeting planner's job in relation to other jobs. Discover what those standards are. If you are performing professionally as a meeting planner, you should rate very high in the hierarchy. If you do not, two problems may prevail: First, you may *not* be doing a high-level job; second, you *are* doing a high-level job but are not being recognized for it because you have failed to properly educate the "powers-that-be."

Have patience! Remember that meeting planning is a newly emerging profession with no generally accepted standard of performance. It is also difficult to compare any given meeting planner's job with another's in another company or association. With such ambiguity present, you can surely recognize how difficult it is to compare a meeting planner's job with other jobs—such as that of a marketing vice president—in the organization which already have clear job descriptions.

Work on this problem by pointing out the following factors to company or association management:

(1) Travel time for the meeting planner is different from travel time for other executives.

Travel time and weeks on the road for the typical traveling executive are based on a Monday through Friday schedule. But for the meeting planner travel time frequently involves weekend time in addition to the traditional work week.

To illustrate: a typical meeting requiring on-the-spot supervision usually runs from Sunday through Wednesday or from Wednesday through Saturday. Often such meetings incorporate early arrival VIP activities. To do the job properly, the meeting planner must arrive *before* scheduled activities begin and remain *after* for vital accounting reviews and other follow-up activities. The result is a heavy weekend workload and often a seven day work week.

(2) The meeting planner must also function within the traditional executive job environment.

Weekend work is often necessary to accommodate the overall organizational system and environment in which the planner must perform when not traveling. The everyday organizational paper flow is more than enough to require Saturday, and often Sunday, work just to keep up with it. And because the planner is so often on the road, he or she has the added burden of catching up with what went on while gone from the office.

(3) The meeting planning executive's work day is longer and different.

Most executives work hard, long hours. Recognition and compensation programs reflect this. But despite the potentially attractive and pseudo-glamorous work environment, the meeting planner's work day during a meeting is far longer—and quite different—than that of other executives in the same organization.

The planner works in a strange, foreign environment that changes each week. He or she is on call twenty-four hours a day and may be called upon at any time to deal with diverse emergencies such as medical problems, thefts or unruly guests.

(4) The planner must master complex and sensitive interpersonal relationships.

The planner must simultaneously interrelate with three distinct bodies of people—meeting delegates, organizational management and suppliers of service (hotel people, airline people, audiovisual technicians, etc.).

Each body of people seems to feel that the meeting planner's sole job is to cater to their particular needs. This creates a pressure pot of people and is the prime reason why so many good people leave the field. No other executive works so continuously in such a complex world of people—and the problem is compounded by the ever-changing environment in which the meeting planner must function.

Establish A Written Meeting Policy Statement

A statement of policy for meetings is essential for any effective organization and should be a great benefit to the meeting planner. You can often tell more about an organization's management by its treatment of meetings than you can by its annual report.

An organization that is cancelling meetings that were once firmly scheduled is often one whose management is scared of the future and unsure of the present. Hesitation in the conduct of a meeting is symptomatic of a management team that is unsure of the value of its meetings and of its current ability to solve problems.

On the other hand, an organization with a clearly written policy of the purposes and objectives of its meetings is progressive, confident of the future and looks upon meetings as an investment, an integral part of its way of doing business.

The planner should assist the organization in preparing a written meeting policy statement. This statement should provide good insight into how the organization evaluates the importance of meetings—and, therefore, the planner's job. The policy statement will include items such as:

(1) **Meetings represent a significant investment of dollars and people time.**
(2) **Meetings are an integral part of the organization's business planning process and business strategy.**
(3) **The basic purpose and objectives of all meetings.**
(4) **The frequency of meetings.**
(5) **Attendance guidelines and eligible guests.**
(6) **Post-meeting evaluation procedures.**
(7) **Cost handling guidelines and similar related items.**

A clearly defined policy on meetings should be of great assistance to the meeting planner in establishing credibility, recognition and support within the organization.

III

A MEETING PLANNER'S TEN COMMANDMENTS

There are a number of rules which are essential to a philosophy of meeting management based on the principle that a meeting is an investment of both time and money. Adhere to these rules and it will be a successful investment from the point of view of everyone concerned—your delegates, your company or association . . . and you. I call them the *Ten Commandments of Meeting Planning.*

I. THOU SHALT NOT LET THYSELF GO TO POT

Keep in shape physically before, during and after the meeting—and nervous mental tensions will take care of themselves.

Year-round, engage in a good physical program to keep the muscles supple. Bowling, golf, tennis, squash, brisk walks—even mowing the lawn—are all good.

Remember . . . a meeting planner is usually the first one up in the morning and the last one to bed at night. The planner's day contains 18 to 20 hours of pressure. If you are not normally an early riser, for a few weeks prior to your next major meeting, start getting out of bed each morning at the same time you must rise during your meeting. Your physical and mental systems will then be adjusted in advance to your meeting schedule.

II. THOU SHALT HONOR THY NAP TIME

Every *body* needs rest and it is stupid to try to push the body beyond human endurance.

Late in the afternoon of each day of a meeting, work in an hour or two for complete relaxation of mind and body. As circumstances permit, stretch out in your room, on the beach or at poolside.

If you elect to nap in your room, alert the hotel switchboard that you are not to be disturbed except for emergencies. Give the chief telephone operator a list of those eligible to contact you—your home, your office or VIP's attending the meeting.

Remember, evening activities are the fun part of a meeting for the attendees. They expect everything to run smoothly and efficiently with receptions and dinners starting on time, excellent service, compatible dinner partners—everything operating effortlessly. It is, therefore, extremely important that the meeting planner be rested, alert and totally in control.

III. THOU SHALT NOT BE OBESE

Control your input of fancy food and alcohol. Remember, the meeting you are supervising is for the benefit of your delegates. Too much rich food is apt to make you sluggish—too much alcohol will obviously slow your reflexes.

Thick juicy steaks, baked potatoes swimming in butter and covered with sour cream, vegetables served with a rich creamy sauce, fancy rich desserts are to be anticipated and enjoyed by the delegates who perhaps attend one or two of these meetings a year. But the professional meeting planner who supervises dozens of these meetings each year must become an expert on nutrition and learn to stay away from any rich, fattening dishes served.

As far as drinking too much at a meeting goes, perhaps you'd like to practice my little secret. I'm known as a gin and tonic man; that's all I ever drink. I've been told I must have a hollow leg by some who are amazed at my capacity and stamina for drinking gin and tonics with no apparent effects. Why gin and tonics? Well, as you know, these drinks are colorless and I can easily switch to straight water or club soda without being obvious. Every bartender at every hotel where I am conducting a meeting knows in advance that when Jim

Jones orders a gin and tonic for himself, he is to be served straight water!

Personal discipline in this area is essential. This practice permits me to fully engage in the social environment of my meeting without seeming to disparage the delegates really imbibing. And it is a great asset in helping me to stay *in control.*

IV. THOU SHALT LAY DOWN THY HEAD NEAR WHERE THE ACTION IS

Select your room for your own convenience. Save yourself all the wear and tear possible. You'll want to be in a convenient location to interact with your major service suppliers—the sales manager, convention service manager, front office or meeting room. So do yourself a great favor and choose a room which will save you the greatest amount of running around!

V. HONOR THY OWN TIME AND CONVENIENCE FIRST

Work your own personal schedule while the meeting is going on whether or not this happens to be the normal work schedule of the hotel personnel at your meeting site. Develop a work plan that fits your own personality and work habits, and prior to each meeting notify the hotel personnel as to how you want things done and when you want things done.

Each of us has a time of the day that is best for us to face and solve the problems of that day. The morning hours happen to be my best time of day for digging into small, but important, details of a meeting in progress.

I do not like having any details of my meeting brought to my attention while I am with any of my meeting delegates. Neither do I want to think about such things as reception costs, dinner bills, or any other such master account cost items during my vital nap period in the afternoon. Therefore, before each meeting, I make arrangements with hotel personnel to bring all of the prior day's master account charges to my room early in the morning, before 7:15 a.m. so I am assured of privacy while digging into meeting details at a time when I am sharp and alert. Incidentally, this procedure also works as a built-in double check to make sure I am up in time for activities scheduled for that day.

If at all possible, insist that your meeting room set-up is prepared the night before, and that all visual-aid equipment is working and in proper order.

VI. THOU SHALT NOT BEAR FALSE WITNESS TO THE HOTELS OR THE DELEGATES

A meeting planner may never speak with forked tongue. Delegates must know all the facts and the hotel must know all of the facts. This problem is solved via meeting releases.

The key to correct information to both the hotels and the delegates is a basic meeting release made as comprehensive and attractive as possible. These meeting releases are, of course, prepared basically for the delegates. But in order to make our circle of communication complete, the hotel must also receive copies of this same release.

People read material more thoroughly when emphasized with pictures and bold lettering to emphasize major points. You will find that disciplining yourself in the preparation of advance information to both the hotel and your delegates is a great preventative of possible headaches during the meeting.

VII. THOU SHALT NOT EXERT THYSELF IN VAIN

You are a meeting planner; you are not a jack of all trades. To retain your sanity and maintain your energy and, above all, to end up with a successful meeting, learn how to delegate and buy *real professional service.*

As a meeting planner, you should be the source of procuring all necessary services for your meeting. You are also responsible for getting all pertinent information to your meeting attendees as well as the hotel at which the meeting will be held. Hire yourself an *excellent* staff, not just a *good* staff! Train them to the way that you want things done, and then turn the responsibilities over to them.

Hire out those jobs at the hotel that you shouldn't be doing in the first place. Don't try to be a photographer, a visual-aid operator and a registration clerk; you are a professional meeting planner.

VIII. TO THINE OWN SELF BE TRUE

In order to be loved, you must first love yourself. In order to be respected, you must first respect yourself.

You have a big job, an important one—and you know how to carry it off successfully. Love yourself for it; respect yourself for it!

IX. KNOW THEE THY JOB AND TO THAT ALSO BE TRUE

Your job as a meeting planner is to maximize a corporate or association investment of money and people time in a meeting and to make sure that everything meshes together in complete harmony. Don't get tied up in petty situations and problems that prevent you from doing your major job.

Learn how to excuse yourself from such situations and get on to the important aspects of your job. If you are asked to do things that are not important to the success of your job, don't do them!

Don't become an individual vacation consultant or a source of special favors! Do learn to treat all people equally, with no special treatment for anyone. Give to one and all the high level of service that relates to the specific objective of the meeting!

X. KEEP HOLY THE SERVE-FIRST PHILOSOPHY

Honor not the wishes of the meeting attendee who covets his neighbor's room or seat at the dinner table. Play no favorites!

Be consistent, and keep in perspective that you are essentially providing a service that demands high standards of service on your part. All people attending your meeting expect equal consideration and top performance from you. When they get it, you are doing your job!

Develop a modus operandi that fits your personality and the tone of your company. Once you have this accomplished, stay on the track! As you continue to grow, you will find that the positive rewards of your job far outweigh any negatives!

And so . . . blessed be the meeting planner who follows the ten commandments of meeting planning for he or she shall inherit the secret of being able to walk away after a meeting with a feeling of exhilaration and a sense of well-being—with pride in a job well done!

IV

PURPOSE
AND OBJECTIVE

Establishment of the purpose and objective of a meeting is the first, most critical step in professional meeting management. Without a clearly defined purpose and objective, planning an effective business program, at best an elusive, complex task, can become an impossible one.

> **A meeting's overall purpose may be educational, informational, motivational—or any combination of these approaches. The objective, on the other hand, should be specific and preferably measure-able in some tangible way.**

Both the purpose and the objective should be up-to-date or the result will be a traditional business program in a format that fails to meet the current needs of either the meeting's delegates or the sponsoring organization. So, carefully research the needs and desires of both company or association and potential delegates to the meeting under consideration.

Defining Purpose And Objective

A well-developed **purpose** for a meeting might be: *To give our newer agents a sense of belonging to a large national company; and to give them a concise review of our sales process to assure their being on track as far as work habits and prescribed sales procedure are concerned.*

The **objectives** in this case might be: *To improve the company's retention rate; and to accelerate the personal production of these men and women.*

The concept of purpose and objective is easily grasped if you look at it in terms of professional meeting planning. The **purpose** of a meeting planner is to plan effective, meaningful meetings. The **objective** of a meeting planner is to maximize the return on dollars and people time invested in meetings.

Think of the meeting's purpose and objectives as the rudder of a ship—without them you are in for a stormy sail to nowhere. To make this rudder as true and precise an instrument of navigation as possible, the purpose and objectives should be agreed upon, clearly understood, written down and referred to whenever a question arises. They should be defined before any other aspect of preparation for a meeting—no matter how basic—is undertaken.

Once clearly defined, the purpose and objectives will be used as guides in site selection, budget preparation and all other components of meeting management. The greatest benefit, however, is in the selection and utilization of people who will make presentations at the meeting. Speakers, instructors, educators and top company or association officials who will be involved in the program should be selected according to their ability to fit into the program and to enhance and further the meeting's objectives.

PROGRAM AND SPEAKER SELECTION

The persons who will make presentations during the meeting should be carefully selected and screened for their ability to communicate and educate.

Don't Assume

Be particularly careful not to fall into the trap of assuming—as one might in the case of an agency force sales meeting—that super achievers will be super educators or super speakers. More frequently they are not! This type of individual, by the very nature of his or her success, often lives in quite a different world and does things that your typical salesperson cannot or should not be doing for a multitude of reasons—not the least of which are lack of experience and/or lack of technical knowledge.

It is often far better to select successful people who are closer to the delegate or student body in terms of length of time in the business rather than super achievers who have a hard time "remembering when." It is easier for an audience to relate to someone who is *closer* to them.

This should not be taken to mean that the very highest achievers cannot be used in business meeting programming, rather that they must be used selectively and appropriately. To illustrate: If you are conducting a training meeting for salespeople who have been in the business less than two years, it would be effective to have a "big-hitter" start the meeting off in the role of philosopher. His job would be to set a high tone and issue a motivational message on behalf of your company and industry. He should, however, be kept out of the "nuts and bolts" of data taking and prospecting.

A "big-hitter" can also be used at the close of the program to offer a challenge to the newer agents to put to work the new ideas and tools they have acquired during the training sessions. The super achiever will exemplify what the newer agents might become.

Avoid Politics And Egos

Beware of and avoid political considerations which are frequently brought to bear in the selection of speakers to make presentations: "John must be on the program because he is president of the company or head of the department." Ego gratification creeps in too: "Pete should be in that slot because, after all, he is the leading salesman."

Speaker selection in these cases becomes an amenity; and

programming of this sort is unfair to the speaker as well as the audience. Inevitably, the speaker assumes that his selection was based on the needs of the business program. He devotes considerable time and energy to his presentation, and only after the fact realizes that it was a wasted effort. Such programming should be eliminated, and the most effective tool for doing so is the written purpose and objective.

Purpose and *objective* must be the key factors in selecting speakers and making other decisions relative to the business program. With a well thought-out purpose and objective serving as the rudder, a meeting planner finds smooth sailing to any destination.

Part Two

BEFORE THE MEETING: MECHANICS AND METHODS

V

SITE SELECTION

It is a difficult task to choose the right location for a conference or convention. Many decisions have to be made. Should you use a domestic or a foreign site? a resort or a downtown commercial hotel? a cruise ship? a conference center? an airport hotel? or your home office?

Due to time and monetary limitations, it is impossible for the meeting planner to personally inspect each and every property that might satisfactorily fulfill his or her conference requirements. Unfortunately, this often leads—unnecessarily—to a non-objective, unbusinesslike approach to site selection; and decisions are made which result in unsatisfactory meetings and/or last minute cancellations.

Despite the problems of a fragmented marketplace, however, planners can develop a systematic approach to site selection which will save time, money and the agony of conducting a meeting at a site that is inappropriate. Ideally, the four phases of the site selection process should include: consultation and data gathering; pre-screening of potential sites; site inspection; and finally, hotel negotiations.

CONSULTATION AND DATA GATHERING

The data gathering phase is of prime importance to good, efficient site selection. It takes place within your own organization and must be done *thoroughly*.

Meeting Purpose and Objective

A meeting's *purpose* may be to educate, to motivate or to inform. The *objective,* on the other hand, should be specific and preferably measurable in some way. Both purpose and objective should be written down, agreed upon and understood.

The reasons *why* the meeting is being conducted and *what you are trying to accomplish* should be a major determinant of *where* you meet. To illustrate: If the purpose of the meeting is to explain next year's compensation program—and your objective is to do this quickly and conveniently, cutting sales time loss to a minimum—then you should logically consider an airport facility central to the population of your meeting delegates. But if you are dealing with a serious educational program, you should probably consider a conference center or your home office location.

Proposed Attendance

The size of your meeting is of vital importance. If it is in the 50-100 people range, your options are many. But if your meeting is very large, two or three thousand people, your options are obviously limited.

Budget Limitations

You must determine your "ballpark" budget figure before you can approach site selection intelligently. While it is true that you cannot prepare a final budget until your site has actually been selected, you must know how much of an investment your company is willing to make. If you have the money, your site selection opportunities are diverse; but if you don't, the choices are obviously limited.

As basic as this may seem, many last minute cancellations are the result of the planner's failure to ascertain the maximum allowable budget expenditure *before* booking a meeting. Determine how much you are willing to spend per day on hotel charges. Once you establish this maximum, you will not waste time looking at luxury hotels when the budget calls for more economy.

Transportation costs, which typically range from 40% to 60% of the total meeting budget should be carefully evaluated from both an expense and a time viewpoint. *Are you willing to spend the dollars and people time to get there?*

Program Criteria

Establish a clear understanding of the maximums as they relate to your business program. Questions that *must* be answered before meaningful site selection can begin are:

How many hours per day are you going to be in formal business sessions?

If you are planning business meetings all day from 8 a.m. to 5 p.m., don't choose a resort with great facilities for golf, tennis, swimming and other potential distractions.

What is your expected maximum attendance for general assembly business sessions?

What is the maximum number of breakout rooms you will require?

You should also determine in advance your basic requirements for your social program.

Are there going to be private receptions each evening?

Do you desire a theme party or private dinner dance one evening?

Are special spouse and/or children's programs required?

Legal Restrictions

Know the laws and federal regulations that relate to your industry. They could have an effect on your site selection. New York State insurance laws, for example, prohibit the use of cruise ships for agent meetings. Since my company is licensed to do business in New York, it is obviously my responsibility to know this and not book a cruise ship for an agents' meeting. Likewise, all meeting planners should keep up with the latest renderings of the Tax Reform Act.

Company Politics

Everyday office politics can play a role in site selection. For example, your company may have an investment in hotel properties in the geographical area under consideration.

Become aware of all the internal, political complications that could affect your decision. These may or may not prevail, but if they do, it is better to know about them in advance rather than after the fact. It is even possible that special rules, influences or guidelines are so cumbersome that meaningful site selection is impossible. If this is so, the problem should be described in writing to a top company authority.

All of these data gathering steps are essential in the first phase of planning a successful meeting. They serve as good eliminators on what could be a very long list. Once the list has been purged, the planner has a more manageable number of options to consider.

PRE-SCREENING OF POTENTIAL SITES

A repeat location is always easier to work than a new one; so if there is a site which you have already used which can do the job, by all means meet there. If there is not, you should do as much pre-screening and research as possible before making even one phone call to a potential meeting site.

Select a site that will meet the needs of the meeting under consideration as well as others you might conduct in the future. Remember the golden rule of site selection:

Never look at or book a hotel you plan on using only once.

It is too expensive; and the loss of the ability to apply experience to future meetings should eliminate the site from further consideration.

PRE-SCREENING RESOURCES

Numerous research facilities and techniques are available to you as a meeting planner to assist you in reducing the enormous number of potential sites to a manageable few. The following is a list of resources that can be used.

Discussion With Other Meeting Planners
The very best source of a reliable, objective evaluation of a potential conference site is someone you know. This is where membership in the meeting planning associations—like Meeting Planners International or the Insurance Conference Planners Association—can be extremely helpful. The greatest benefit of active participation in these organizations is the opportunity to learn from the experience of others.

Contacting Hotel Associates
Discussion with hotel associates not in line for your current business is one of the most effective ways to screen a property. Frequently, they know the key personnel at other meeting sites as well as the facilities. And if you have worked successfully with them in the past, they also know how you work as well as what you need and expect.

Hotel and Supplier Correspondence Files
General hotel correspondence, brochures and other information should be filed away for future use. In my office, we file such items alphabetically by state. We also clip advertisements that catch our eye. Those hotels and resorts that advertise *want* your business.

Business Publications
Many of the meeting trade publications—*Insurance Conference Planner, Meetings & Conventions, Successful Meetings* and *Meeting News,* to name a few—publish concise, valuable area guides. They

not only list potential meeting sites and their capabilities but provide useful information on weather, modes of dress, sightseeing highlights and airline service that you can incorporate into your advance meeting information.

Contact the editors and publishers of these magazines for more assistance and detailed information on potential sites. They are well acquainted with many sites because by the nature of their business they have traveled to many meetings and spoken with many hotel people. They provide objective, useful information and are one of the best pre-screening sources.

There are a number of directories of meeting facilities published annually. They are: The *Official Hotel and Motel Directory and Facilities Guide* published by the Hotel Sales Management Association; the *Hotel and Motel Red Book* by the American Hotel and Motel Association; the *Official Meeting Facilities Guide* by Ziff-Davis Publishing Co.; the *Annual Gavel Directory* by *Meetings and Conventions* magazine; and the *International Facilities Directory* by *Successful Meetings* magazine.

Convention and Visitors Bureaus

The convention bureaus of various locales have a wealth of information that can be sent to you without obligation. They are also excellent sources of free promotional material.

Hotel Representatives

If you are considering one of their properties, a hotel representative can help. Keep in mind, however, that they will be pushing one of the properties they represent and may not be able to give a truly objective evaluation.

Several groups, most notably the Krisam Group and Robert F. Warner Inc., have done a fine job of expanding the role of hotel representatives. They offer high caliber meeting planning assistance to those who use their properties; and they also publish directories of their hotels' facilities.

Major Hotel Chains' National Sales Offices

In actual practice, personnel in these offices are similar to hotel representatives. They can assist in pre-screening of their properties but be careful that you don't trigger an avalanche of mail and solicitations from other chain properties. Explain that you are simply seeking data and do not want a firm proposal at this time.

All major chains—Marriott, Hilton, Sheraton, Holiday Inns, Trust Houses Forte, Western International—offer free directories or fact finders listing all their properties with housing statistics and other useful information. Be sure to get your name on the mailing lists of these major chains.

Smaller Hotel Organizations

Some of the organizations of smaller hotels—like AIRCOA—provide free data on member properties. Don't overlook some of these booklets; often they are gems.

Airlines

Check with your airline sales office, particularly if the airline services the area you are considering with a large number of flights. Frequently someone in the sales office will know the area well and be able to provide you with objective information. Airlines are also a handy source of free promotional material for your meeting information release.

Meeting Evaluation Reports From Past Meetings

The results you have had with past meetings—if documented by formal post-meeting evaluation—serve as a *very* useful tool for internal site selection purposes.

Other People Within Your Company

If you know of employees in your company who have knowledge of the site under consideration, ask for their opinion. This is not the best source of pre-screening information, but at least you can get some kind of feel for the property in advance of an inspection visit.

The pre-screening phase might be considered as qualifying the prospect. If you have done your job professionally you should now be in a position to place a phone call to a hotel sales manager to check on desired dates and availability of basic facilities. Your pre-screening continues with this initial phone call. You are not only seeking desired dates and proposed rates, you are continuing your evaluation of the hotel.

After your call you must ask yourself some questions: How did the hotel operator respond to your request to speak to "Mr. Sales Manager?" Did she sound as if she knew him? Was she courteous? How did the sales manager's secretary respond? Was the sales manager enthusiastic on the phone?

Take this opportunity to learn about the hotel's management and prior track record with business groups. Ask such questions as: Who is the general manager? What is his background? How long has the sales manager been there? Who will service your meeting if it is booked? Do they have a conference service staff?

What other groups are in the hotel during the time you are considering? What groups like yours have they recently serviced? Whom can you contact from such groups for a referral?

The point is—ask questions that you feel are important *before* setting up a mutually convenient date for an inspection visit. If these questions are not answered to your satisfaction and in a businesslike manner, forget the inspection visit and look elsewhere.

SITE INSPECTION

Since the purpose of your site inspection visit is to get a feel for the hotel, evaluate hotel management and determine if the property has the service and facilities to make your meeting a success, the visit should be conducted at a mutually convenient time for you and the key hotel personnel—the general manager and the director of sales.

While there are many ways for planners to approach this situation, the following is the method of site inspection with which I have had greatest success.

Typical Room

In general, your inspection tour will require no more than two evenings at the hotel. Make sure that you are registered in a room that is typical of the one to which your average delegate will be assigned, not a VIP suite.

Check List

Use a meeting check list, such as the standard one developed by the Insurance Conference Planners Association which is printed in the back of this book, and send two copies to the hotel in advance of your visit. Request that one copy be completed by them and held at the registration desk for your arrival.

Viewpoints In Advance

If you have any special meeting philosophy, it is best expressed early. You will assist the hotel's management in preparing for your visit by communicating any distinct convictions you have on sensitive subjects like gratuities or negotiations in advance.

Typical Travel

It is best that you experience the same type of travel situation your delegates will face getting from the airport to the hotel, so do not let the hotel make special arrangements to meet you.

Get A Feel For The Property

Try to arrive the afternoon of the day preceding your official appointment so that you have an opportunity to get a feel for the hotel. Talk with other guests; discover why they selected this hotel, how they like it, what they think of the food, how they rate the service and the attitude of the staff. These are often very helpful perceptions.

You should experience firsthand the service put forth by the hotel's staff—limousine drivers, bellmen, doorman, registration clerks, waiters, golf and tennis pros, pool boys, maids—without the hotel's management present and without letting the staff know who you are and why you are there. A great deal can be learned during this personal observation. Take note: Is the staff neatly attired? clean?

friendly? Is their attitude courteous? Do they have a sense of pride in their work?

Having dinner alone the first evening, you can casually review the menu, wine list, prices, staff complement, acoustics, type of music played, dancing facilities, etc. Back in your room, in peace and quiet, you can go over the occurrences of the day. Was your meeting check list neatly and completely filled out? Was it waiting for you at the registration desk upon your arrival as you requested? Is the hotel clean and well maintained? Does it have the basic physical plant to do the job that you require?

Official Meeting

Set your first important meeting for 9 a.m. with the general manager and the director of sales. The time is indicative of a businesslike approach, and this is a vitally important business meeting.

You want to see how the general manager's office is run. You also want to take note: Was he friendly? punctual? What was the relationship between the general manager and the director of sales? Are they at ease with one another? with you?

Of course, you should be respectful of the general manager's time, but there are a number of basic subjects which *must* be covered. To begin with, make it clear that you are a professional meeting planner, not a travel agent. Be sure they know that your business is direct business, non-commissionable to any person or source, and that therefore you buy only net rates for your meetings.

Next, you want them to understand that since this visit is being conducted at considerable expense to your company or association, you will appreciate being able to spend the next three or four hours with the sales manager *uninterrupted.* You also want to ascertain that the sales manager is authorized to make commitments in all areas of negotiations because you do not want to waste time discussing subjects which must be taken up with the general manager.

Now, at last, you place yourself in the hands of the sales manager and inspect all aspects of the hotel. Ask to be introduced to as many key department heads as possible . . . and ask a lot of questions.

What are the three major strengths of this hotel? What are its three major weaknesses? What are they doing to correct them? What unique ideas for theme parties or social activities can they offer?

When a site, for whatever reason, appears not to be right, stop the inspection process immediately and explain your thinking to both the general manager and the sales manager. They will appreciate knowing why you didn't buy; and perhaps it will be useful to them in correcting the problem before another planner rejects them for a similar reason.

A site inspection without a potential piece of business to book and negotiate is an extravagant waste of time for all parties concerned. But if you have done a good, professional job of pre-screening and qualifying a prospective meeting site, you should very infrequently have to reject a site before moving into the next phase—basic negotiation.

VI

HOTEL NEGOTIATIONS

Negotiating the arrangements for an intended meeting is the final, fourth phase of site selection and one of the key responsibilities of the professional meeting planner. Before you give a final "yes" or "no" to a site, basic negotiations must be completed. But while there is no mystery about this bargaining procedure, it is often made more complicated than it really is. Quite simply, you must know *what* to negotiate, *when* and *where* to negotiate and with *whom*. And before you can begin to negotiate successfully you must have a clear understanding of the *quality* of your business.

QUALITY OF BUSINESS

The *quality* of your particular piece of business—of your total meeting—is the *total potential income* from it to the hotel. In most cases this involves far more than rooms and meals.

The hotel is, of course, in business to make money. You, on the other hand, are looking for the best possible price and service for your group. When you have ascertained the net worth of your business to the hotel, then you are in a position to bargain for the service that will truly make yours a successful meeting.

Measuring Quality

A definition of the quality of your meeting should include the following factors:

Number of people

Type of people—their income level and spending habits

Length of stay—arrival and departure pattern

Type of program—sponsored receptions, dinners, recreational activities

Room Occupancy pattern—a high percentage of double occupancies is a plus in the planner's favor

Expense accounts—are guests to be on expense accounts or not?

There may be other factors that would be meaningful in the measurement of quality for this particular meeting. But the important thing to keep in mind is . . .

> **If your group has a high income profile—as far as the hotel's assessment of the profit it will provide— then you are in a strong negotiating position.**

A knowledge of accounting techniques and procedures can also be used as a negotiating tool. And by recognizing hotel dollar flow patterns and effectively using advance deposits and guarantees, you can greatly enhance your bargaining position.

For an example of such bargaining leverage, consider the following: Simply by instructing meeting delegates to pay all hotel charges either in cash or by personal check, you can save the hotel up to seven percent in credit card charges. Moreover, you have eliminated the need for hotel to maintain city ledger accounts, thus saving untold administration costs. By placing an association or corporate guarantee on personal checks covering hotel expenses, you can add even more to your bargaining power.

Communicate your knowledge of and willingness to employ

techniques such as the above to the hotel's management. They'll listen! And now you are ready to really negotiate.

WHAT TO NEGOTIATE

Of course, it is important to negotiate prices, but too often the meeting planner places far too much emphasis on price negotiations. He or she gets all hung up on basic hotel rates or complimentary cocktail parties, forgetting that such factors are, in the long run, only a small part of the total package. Price should never be the prime determinant of a meeting site—and direct dollar expenditure alone should never be the measurement of successful negotiations with a hotel.

What should the planner negotiate first?

It is imperative for the meeting planner to negotiate first for SERVICES and FACILITIES that will assure the success of the meeting.

In no way do I mean to downplay the importance of direct dollar negotiation; I simply feel that things should be kept in their proper perspective. No matter how good a deal a meeting planner is able to negotiate on total cost, a meeting is doomed from the beginning without excellent facilities and services. Ideally, you should seek a blend and balance of services, facilities and price that are everything you need for a successful meeting and a fair and reasonable agreement for all parties concerned—your company or association *and* the hotel.

A telescopic concept of hotel negotiations as revolving only around price indicates an inexperienced planner—or worse still, an ineffective and non-professional one. Here are just a few examples which illustrate the importance of negotiating services and facilities *before* you get into the subject of price.

Services

Is the normal bell staff complement sufficient to meet your

standards for moving your guests efficiently and rapidly in and out of the hotel? If not, negotiate in advance for a specific additional number of people to handle your group—and get the number in writing. If you do eventually book with this hotel, check again at a later date to be sure that the hotel has gone through with the arrangement.

Does the check-in time for your group correspond with that of the arrival or departure of another large group? If the answer is "yes," negotiate for extra maid and housekeeping personnel to expedite your check-in. Agree to numbers—and be sure to get them in writing. You might also negotiate for extra accounting staff to expedite your group's check-out; or make provisions for separate check-out facilities if you deem it necessary. At least, make sure a decision maker from the accounting department is available to straighten out any problems on the spot.

What are the hotel's food and beverage service standards for a group the size of yours? Do they meet your standards? Be sure to negotiate the number of bars, bartenders, waiters and waitresses you need. This is an excellent example of service being more important than price. You could spend hours trying to have the hotel lower the price of a drink—and even if you succeed, you will have won nothing if your guests can't be served!

How about the total staff complement for meal functions? Be sure to negotiate the numbers of waiters and waitresses and captains as carefully as you do the basic price of the meal and applicable surcharges. Have you ever been served in a hotel where the staffing standard calls for one waiter per twenty customers? I have and I didn't appreciate the service one bit! In advance of a firm booking, this item can easily be negotiated to a more acceptable one waiter per every ten guests dining on a set menu.

Facilities

Prior to making a firm commitment, negotiate for the space you will need for this meeting. Don't assume anything! Make sure the hotel actually has enough space for your needs and that it will be available at the time of your meeting. Then negotiate.

Now is the time to negotiate specific golf starting times that blend into your social/business program hours. This may be more important than the basic group greens fee you agree to. After all, what good is a low greens fee if you can't get on the course?

The same principle applies to tennis. Those low court rental fees or courts with the compliments of the hotel won't be of any use to your attendees if the courts are being used during their free time.

Room Block

The *room block* is a simple area for hard negotiation. Don't overlook it!

First, determine the quality of rooms in the hotel. A good indication of room quality is very often the hotel's "rack rate," the cost of any given room. Use this as a guide, but be sure to personally inspect each type of room and make your own value judgments.

How do the rooms stack up? How many would you consider deluxe? How many standard? How many below standard? Grade the rooms into meaningful and understandable categories such as A, B, C, D. By determining what percentage of your rooms will be in each category, you can establish the quality of your room block.

Now you are all set to negotiate for a high quality block of rooms at a fair and reasonable price! And negotiating in this vital area is always a challenge for the professional meeting planner!

COSTS TO NEGOTIATE

Companies and associations expect excellent facilities and services as a matter of course for all meetings. On the other hand, each meeting is budgeted, and it is the meeting planner's responsibility to get those high quality services and facilities *and* stay within the budget. Money does talk, and, in the final analysis, the cost of the meeting is what the management listens to.

There are five areas of direct cost that should be negotiated. In order of importance, they are: basic hotel rates, reception costs, gratuities, recreation costs and miscellaneous costs.

Basic Hotel Rates

It is absoutely mandatory that a meeting planner learn to analyze hotel rate structure. What many hotels call a *group rate,* for instance, is merely an illusion. The buyer, on hearing this term, naturally assumes that he is getting a lower rate than an individual would pay. But often, under closer scrutiny, the so-called *group rate* turns out to be nothing more than an average run-of-the-house rate.

Don't fall into this trap! Investigate and compare the group quote you are given with applicable individual rates. If an individual can walk in and get a room for x amount of dollars, are you going to pay more for that room in your group rate?

Ask the hotel for a *volume rate.* Don't be surprised if the management isn't familiar with the term. You will have to go on and explain that since you are dealing with a volume of room reservations, you naturally assume you will be given a rate lower than that which the individual guest pays. The answer is inevitable: "Yes, your assumption is correct." And now you are in a position to negotiate a true volume rate, a *legitimate group rate.*

Learn the difference between a *gross rate* (which includes a commission factor) and a *net rate* (cost to the direct buyer) and let the hotel's management know that you know the difference. If you are a direct buyer, make it very clear that business you are booking is under no circumstances commissionable. By so doing you have added another item to your tangibles for negotiating a fair and reasonable volume (group) rate.

Reception Costs

Liquor is a high profit item for a hotel and should be high on the list of prices to negotiate. If you are sponsoring several receptions, thus greatly increasing the *quality* of your business, try to develop a sliding price scale for drinks—based on the entire meeting time period, not on a reception to reception basis. Negotiate to establish a cumulative reduction of unit price for drinks based on total expected liquor consumption. In other words, *seek a volume discount.*

You are apt to have a tough fight on your hands on this point, for it is a key area for hard negotiating. If you cannot come to complete agreement with management on liquor prices, try negotiating for a reduction of costs in other areas relative to liquor consumption— costs such as orchestras or entertainment.

Gratuities

Gratuity handling has a major cost impact on a meeting and should therefore be an area for direct negotiation. Make sure that every dollar will be distributed fairly and honestly to the people who have earned it. (For a thorough discussion of gratuity disbursement, see Chapter XXI.)

Recreation Costs

Very often it is possible to negotiate for a group rate on greens fees, tennis court time, horseback riding and pool facilities. This is especially true if you are willing to get into some form of organizational sponsorship of activities, such as golf or a tennis tournament.

It is important that you apply the concept of volume buying to recreational activities as well. With a large volume input to the hotel, why not a cost break to you? Evaluate proposed recreational costs as they relate to the basic hotel costs you are paying. Recreation costs should be reasonable enough so that they do not serve as an irritant to your people. So be sure you do not negate an otherwise good job of negotiation in the less visible areas by failure to bargain for a reasonable price for recreation.

Miscellaneous Costs

What else will you be spending on? Many incidentals will crop up—coffee breaks, room set-ups, security, visual aid support, account preparation. These miscellaneous items require negotiation too. Think about what you need; then get to work!

WHEN TO NEGOTIATE

There's not much sense in locking the barn door after the horse has been stolen. Neither does it make sense for a meeting planner to try to negotiate after he confirms his specific selection of a meeting site. Once you have made a firm booking, hotel management holds all the cards, and you are in no position to bargain.

Willy Sutton, the famous bank robber and professional gunslinger once said, "You get more done with a few kind words and a gun than with a few kind words alone." When negotiating before booking, your "gun" is the ability to refuse to buy, to walk away and to shop elsewhere.

As to the best time to negotiate, I have found that

The extremes—very early (perhaps three or four years in advance) or very late (six months to a year in advance)—are the best times to get exactly what you want.

By booking well in advance you can usually firm up a very reasonable room rate. But because of the wide fluctuation of food prices, never attempt to firm up a full rate (a rate that includes meals) on a long-range basis. This would not be a fair and reasonable request to those hotels operating on a *full* or *modified American* plan rate basis.

If the hotel will not quote a comparatively firm basic room rate this far in advance of your meeting, think twice about making a long-range firm commitment with that particular hotel.

At the other extreme, you may be given a large meeting to plan with only a very short lead time for booking, say six months to a year. If you find a hotel with sufficient space available to service your meeting, you will be in an excellent position to negotiate. With such a short time left for management to gamble on filling these dates at prime rates, they will, no doubt, be anxious to negotiate to get some firm money in the till.

The time period between the first and second extremes seems to be the weakest, the most difficult time for the professional meeting planner to operate.

WHERE TO NEGOTIATE

The most logical and best place to negotiate is at the meeting site under consideration.

Having made an appointment to meet with both the general manager and the sales manager on a specific day, plan to arrive the evening before the scheduled date so you will get a good night's rest. You will want to be physically and mentally alert for the negotiating session. Plan to meet both the general manager and the sales manager at 9 a.m., a time which indicates that you are a businessperson!

WHO SHOULD NEGOTIATE

You, the professional meeting planner should negotiate directly with the sales manager and the general manager of the property.

Some meeting planners allow a company vice president or local representative of their company to look at a facility and make the final decision as to whether it should be used for a particular meeting. This is ludicrous, for good meeting planning is a profession which requires a lot of training and on-the-spot experience. There is no room for amateurs!

Why should the general manager be there? Because you will want him to know exactly what you will be discussing and negotiating with the sales manager—every subject outlined in this chapter.

You will want to ascertain right from the beginning if the sales manager is authorized to make firm commitments in *all* these areas of negotiation. If the sales manager does not have this authorization, then negotiate directly with the general manager.

Even though a sales manager may be authorized to make all major decisions, there is, more often than not, some problem that he will have to discuss with the general manager.

CONTRACTS

Lasting business relationships, like marriages, are built on mutual respect and trust. A formal, standardized contract is not the key to successful meetings. What *is* necessary is an honest, business-like approach on the part of the buyer as well as the seller—a mutual understanding of the needs and objectives of each.

When booking meetings, a hotel operator's biggest problem is *heavy shrinkage*—last minute cancellations and fewer people show up than promised. The buyer's biggest concerns are the room block and the necessary public space, meeting facilities and services—and price variations thereof.

Open Communication

Maintaining open lines of communication between buyer and seller and establishing a formal, mutually agreed upon channel and timetable for future communication eliminate any need for a uniform contract. Trying to cover every contingency gets planners too bogged down in administrative detail; and a piece of paper, after all, is only as good as the two people who have drawn it up.

Place more emphasis on the people with whom you are dealing. Are they knowledgeable? Are they using consulting sales techniques? What is their reputation in the meeting marketplace? (Don't be afraid to ask other planners.) Are they people of integrity?

Commitment

Everything you and the hotel's sales management have discussed can be confirmed by means of a letter documenting the negotiations and your expectations. Follow through with contact at regular intervals.

Remember, good people—staff and service—are the key to successful meetings. Success and a good working relationship, in turn, generate loyalty. Your repeat booking and active good will are the greatest testimony to a job well done by the hotel.

VII

TRAVEL ARRANGEMENTS

Every meeting planner, regardless of the type of organization with which he or she is associated or the reimbursement procedures they follow, must pay close attention to travel arrangements for conference and convention delegates. Adequate transportation is a major determinant—from the standpoint of expense, time and convenience —of the success or failure of a meeting.

For a typical corporate meeting, transportation costs may be as much as 40 to 60 percent of the total budget and are generally absorbed by the company. For an association meeting, on the other hand, each delegate is usually responsible for all personal travel costs; and so convenience and expense are even more critical to a convention's attendance—and thus, ultimately, to its success.

The availability of good transportation is one of the vital criteria for meeting site selection. No matter how well equipped or attractive, if you cannot get delegates to and from a property conveniently and economically, think twice before using it.

THE PLAN

1. Before confirming a meeting site, establish *in writing* a basic travel plan to get all meeting delegates there and back.
2. Keep the plan simple and easy to explain!
3. Base the plan on existing commercial means of travel—airline, train or motor coach.
4. Evaluate the plan both from the standpoint of cost and from the standpoint of convenience and time involved.

    (Evaluate the proposed plan in relation to *all* delegates so as to be aware in advance of any problem situations likely to arise from the few delegates who must go through "travel gymnastics" to get there.)
5. Plan the on-site business and social programs in a way that does not overburden the local travel services *or* your own staff's capability to coordinate and supervise.

To illustrate the degree of advance transportation arrangement that is necessary, let us briefly run through some typical meeting sites and the travel plans that would be practical for them.

Major City Or Suburban Hotel—With Commercial Airport and Limousine Service

Some of the most popular meeting hotels in the country are located in the Phoenix, Arizona area. Excellent transportation via regularly scheduled commercial flights contribute to its popularity and, from the travel plan perspective, the planner's job is easy. Delegates are simply instructed to fly into Phoenix and provided with information on hotel limousine service, taxi cab rates and car rental services available at the airport.

Remote Resort—With Hospitality Gathering Points At Major Airports And Motor Coach To Final Destination

Some excellent meeting sites are not near major commercial airports. The Lake of the Ozarks area is a good example. Resort hotels here are approximately 170 miles southwest of St. Louis and 170 miles southeast of Kansas City. I have conducted many successful meetings in this locale, and my travel plan—which is simple, efficient and very economical — is as follows:

1. Delegates *west* of the Lake of the Ozarks fly into Kansas City. A hospitality gathering point is set up at an airport motel which offers complimentary connection from the airport.
2. Delegates *east* of the Lake of the Ozarks fly into St. Louis where a similar hospitality gathering point is appointed.
3. All delegates are informed of designated motor coach departures from their respective gathering points so that they can arrange flight reservations accordingly.
4. For the bus trip, libations, song sheets and a tour presentation are provided so that travel time passes swiftly.

Local Regional Resort—With No Commercial Transportation

Sometimes site selection is too limited to apply the "availability of travel service" rule. A good site for a regional meeting may be central to the major delegate population but not accessible via commercial means.

Such a destination is the Pocono mountain area in Pennsylvania where I held my Eastern Region's President's Club, an annual meeting for 300-400 delegates and spouses. Ninety percent of the qualifiers are from offices located within a 500-mile radius. A mileage allowance for use of private automobile is the proper basic travel plan for this meeting.

1. **Delegates from offices within a 500-mile radius** are given driving instructions and mileage approximations in an advance release utilizing information provided by the American Automobile Association. Delegates are granted a mileage allowance based on corporate standards plus a miscellaneous allowance for luggage handling, tolls and incidental expenses. Once again, the basic travel plan is simple and easy to explain.
2. **Delegates from offices outside a 500-mile radius** are given a commercial airfare allowance to and from Allentown, Pennsyl-

vania, the nearest city with commercial flight service. These delegates are also given a miscellaneous allowance for connecting limousine, luggage handling and incidental expenses en route.

MODES OF TRANSPORTATION

In addition to regular commercial air service there are other interesting travel alternatives of which the planner should be aware.

Extra Section Flights

Due to demand, an airline may commit to an extra flight which complements the regularly scheduled flight schedule. Commercial air carriers flying a certified air route must use equipment and crews which adhere to high safety and service standards, so extra section flights from these airlines are a good viable alternative for transporting a large group. Be sure, however, to have a written commitment from the airline *before* announcing an extra section flight or saying "yes" to the site for which you need the transportation.

The Marco Beach Hotel on Marco Island, Florida is a good example. If you are taking a large group to this site, Marco Airways must provide sufficient extra section flights to get your whole group to and from Miami—and you should get this commitment *before* you book a group at the hotel. Fortunately, the airline is owned by the same interests as the hotel and cooperation between the two is excellent.

Mackinac Island, Michigan may also necessitate extra section flight planning. This area is serviced very cooperatively by North Central Airlines.

Charter Aircraft

Recent changes in Federal charter regulations have increased the popularity of aircraft charters—and they too can be a convenient and economical way to transport a group. But deal with a reputable airline; and seek assistance from your airline representative or a good travel agent with charter experience.

Train

At one time, train service was a major consideration in meeting travel planning. Times have changed, but with the new equipment and high speed service, train travel should not be excluded from planning. In Canada, Europe and other international destinations, the train remains the efficient, economical and fun way to travel. Always ascertain train service and share this information with your delegates, some of whom may actually prefer this method.

Motor Coach

The word "bus" raises negative connotations; everyone responds better to "motor coach," so use this term in your meeting and travel literature. Whatever the name, it is an economical, efficient mode of transportation. You do not encounter many situations which necessitate a holding pattern and thus it is relatively reliable.

When chartering motor coaches, do not let price alone dictate your choice of company. Deal with a reputable firm that will honor commitments to air conditioning, rest room facilities, luggage rack capacity and back-up crews in the event of heavy demand.

If the ride is to be over an hour, describe it as a "tour." With some imagination on the planner's part, the trip becomes an event and a builder of group feeling and identity. Make the tour a memorable occasion with lunches, drinks, a guitarist, song sheets . . . you name it.

Innovative Transportation

Use your imagination! Unique "travel wrinkles" can get a meeting off to a fast start or a memorable conclusion. Convey delegates on the last leg of the travel plan with canoes, canal barges, horse drawn sleds, carriages, covered wagons, bicycles, English cabs or on horseback—whatever befits the occasion or the locale. Of course, the distance covered in this manner should never be too far.

TRANSPORTATION SUPPLEMENTS

More and more of today's sophisticated meeting delegates need and want auxiliary, private modes of transportation. A complete plan, therefore, will include information on the following, as they pertain to the location of the meeting:

Car Rental Services

Your company or association might be eligible for a volume discount from one of the major car rental firms—Avis, Hertz or National—which have numerous outlets. Discounts can range from 10% to 35% and meeting delegates will always enjoy the savings.

Often, large or well known meeting sites have a major rental company outlet on the premises so that cars can be conveniently dropped off with no extra charge. Delegates will always appreciate this valuable information.

Favorable rates can often be obtained from "off airport" firms such as Thrifty or Budget Car. These rates may be lower than those of the large firms, even including the discount. Also, small local firms frequently offer reliable service at lower cost. All of this, again, is information your delegates will be glad to have.

Nearest Private Airport

With the rapidly increasing demands of time on top executives and guest speakers, as well as the growing affluence of many delegates, more and more people are arriving at meetings via private aircraft. The meeting planner must therefore ascertain the location and specifications of the nearest private airport.

Check for runway length, lighting, control tower, tie down charges, fuel availability—and the types of aircraft that can be safely and conveniently handled. Check too on feasibility and cost of private limousine or taxi service to and from the private airport.

Campsites

Another recent trend is the delegate who drives to the meeting in a camper, so check on parking and service facilities for these vehicles. In addition, it may be helpful to provide information on campsites in the general vicinity of the meeting site for camping delegates who may want to take a little vacation before or after the meeting. This is available from state tourist bureaus.

MEETING ARRIVAL
AND DEPARTURE

To be complete, a travel plan must include hotel check-in and check-out procedures.

Check-In And Room Occupancy

If all delegates are pre-registered, both for the meeting and for hotel rooms, things run much more smoothly on check-in day. To gear their arrival time properly, guests must know when rooms will be available for occupancy.

Paint the picture darker than you actually anticipate. If in your advance planning you determine that, due to maid service turn-around following another large group, the majority of your rooms won't be ready until 2:30 p.m., tell delegates rooms will be available at 3:30 p.m. This builds a time edge in your favor—and I've never heard anyone complain if the room was ready early.

If some delegates must arrive *before* rooms are ready, be sure there is something for them to do. Anticipate their needs and make the unavoidable wait as comfortable as possible. Advise them to pack sports clothes separately so that they can use the recreational facilities while they are waiting for their rooms; and be sure to arrange a private, secure place for changing.

Other conveniences that should be arranged for check-in day are:

Hospitality Center

For every major meeting, a hospitality center should be located as close as possible to the company/association registration center.

In the event of room occupancy delays, delegates will have a comfortable and convenient place to gather, and it is a focal point for renewing old friendships and making new ones.

Registration Center

Delegates should know in advance where to register and how to get there—and whether to report first to the company/association registration center or to the hotel's registration desk.

Message Center

In your registration center, place a message board for delegates to use. Since everyone will be using the registration center at one time or another, it's a good way for delegates to touch bases.

Check-Out And Departure

Hotel check-out and departure from the meeting site present two of the most critical aspects of the travel plan. All the diligent work, effective planning and hard-hitting business and social programming will go for naught if the delegate's departure from the site is not a smooth one. So do the whole job! Don't let up! Get them home as conveniently and comfortably as you brought them to the site.

Double check that agreements concerning the bell staff complement relative to your check-out are honored. **Triple check**—at least one day before—that outgoing travel services are planned for your people.

Make arrangements in advance for speedy VIP check-out. Get prior credit approval. Make sure the hotel's accounting staff and service facilities are geared to your anticipated peak demand times (immediately prior to and immediately following your last day's business or social session).

SOURCES OF ASSISTANCE

When building a travel plan, it is always advisable to seek expert assistance and guidance. The following can be counted upon to help:

1. **Hotel Management**—If they can't explain all the ways to get to and from the hotel, you had better pick another meeting location.
2. **Other Meeting Planners**—Other planners who have used the site will usually share the basic travel plan they used, and even offer suggestions for improving or refining it.
3. **Airlines**—Sales and service personnel for the major connecting airlines can be of help not only with your basic travel plan but also with promotion items such as brochures, program shells and posters.
4. **Convention and Visitors Bureaus**—Tourist organizations are always willing and able to render assistance. They are particularly helpful when working an overseas location. There are no costs for their services.
5. **In-House Travel Departments**—If you have access to such personnel and services, by all means seek assistance and guidance from them.
6. **Incentive Houses**—There are some very good incentive organizations specializing in unique travel programs. They can pass on the benefits of mass purchasing power as well as "know-how."
7. **Professional Travel Agents**—I do not use travel agents in any aspect of my site selection or negotiations. All hotel business placed in behalf of my company is direct and non-commissionable to any person or organization. However, properly used, a travel agent can be a tremendous help. This is particularly true overseas. A good ground operator is a necessity to assist you with city tours, visiting historical sites and moving people from place to place easily and efficiently. Competent agents know the local scene better than you ever will.

   I believe that a meeting planner has a moral obligation to inform or advise delegates on how to get information on any special travel fares to a given destination. Here the travel agent or airline representative can be indispensable.
8. **Local Travel Firms**—A recent trend in the travel support industry has seen the growth of small local firms—often only one or two people—who specialize in children's programs, local area attractions and general meeting support. A group of such firms recently banded together to form a "Convention Service and

Sightseeing Network." Frequently, these organizations work out of a travel agent framework, either on a fee basis or a combination commission/fee basis.

You cannot have a successful meeting without a good travel plan. Nor can you have a successful meeting budget unless you have first worked out a travel plan. It is just that simple. A good travel plan in combination with comprehensive related travel information is indicative of a professional performance. To become a professional, work hard and thoroughly on your transportation and travel arrangements.

VIII

BUDGETING

Budgeting is a helpful—and necessary—frame of reference for completing the final stages of planning a meeting. In fact, meaningful budgeting is impossible without having first worked out an overall meeting plan which fits the basic purpose and objective of a meeting.

Don't put the cart before the horse! Put basic meeting plans—travel, site, business and social programming—in writing. THEN do the budget.

Budgeting need not be complicated. Having assembled the correct information, it is a simple matter of adding up a column of figures.

BUDGET CONSTRUCTION

Attendance
There are two distinct types of company meetings which a planner encounters: invitational meetings sponsored by the company;

or meetings for which attendees must qualify. The type of meeting has a distinct effect on the budget. An invitational or sponsored meeting's attendance is known well in advance. Total numbers can be ascertained simply by adding up the number of invitations issued.

But for a qualification meeting, intelligent guesses (based on last year's qualification figures and including a factor for any special motivating influences) must be made. Association meetings are similar to qualification meetings in that assumptions must be made regarding attendance.

Who Pays For What?

The rules of the game regarding cost are the first step in the budgeting process. What does the company or association pay for? Which items must the delegate pay for? Knowing *who pays for what* is essential to the construction of a meaningful budget. Furthermore, those items for which the delegate is responsible must be clearly explained to the delegate.

THE BUDGETING PROCESS

The following is an illustration of the budgeting process which could be used for a company meeting where all expenses other than recreational costs are paid for by the company:

Travel Plan

Establish and price out a travel plan to and from the meeting site for all delegates.

Room And Board

Determine basic costs for room and board, blanket gratuities and tax based on your assumed attendance and room requirements. This should be an easy task if basic hotel negotiations and planning have been completed.

Business Program

Develop and price by item a business program that accomplishes the meeting's purpose and objectives. Include here: guest speaker's fees; meeting room rental costs; audio-visual support; applicable printed matter; photography costs; and hiring of specialists.

Social Program

Develop and price by item a social program that supports your overall purpose and objectives. Include here: coffee breaks; cocktail parties; special dinners; surcharges; special entertainment; orchestra costs and similar items.

Miscellaneous Items

This is an important part of the budget. Be specific and categorize each item. Include promotional expenses, meeting kits, name badges, shipping charges, special gratuities above basic arrangements—every cost item you can think of. A minimum extra allowance of $2 per delegate—or 10 percent of total miscellaneous items—is also a good idea to build a budgetary edge in your favor.

IX

ADVANCE
COMMUNICATION

The meeting process is a complicated procedure that must be constantly fine-tuned. But the aspect that might contribute most to the delegate's enjoyment of a successful meeting is the *advance information release*. I came to this conclusion after having received numerous evaluations from meeting delegates, hotel people, airline personnel, ground operators and guest speakers. Meeting delegates in particular were most vocal about the need to be well-prepared for a meeting.

> **The attendee has a right to know what to expect; and as a meeting planner it is your responsibility to supply this information.**

Before undertaking to communicate any information to the potential meeting attendee, the nuts and bolts phase of planning the meeting must be complete. You should have firmly nailed down—in writing—the basic program put together with the hotel, the transportation supplier, the audio-visual firm, the guest speakers and the caterer, etc. These are the people who are going to make the meeting work. If that part hasn't been done well, you are not going to do a very good job of communicating with your delegates either.

THE WALK-THROUGH PROCESS

But let us assume that you have accomplished the initial phase. Now it is time to put yourself in the shoes of the meeting delegate—and *walk* him or her through the entire meeting plan. This is what I call the *walk-through process* of meeting management. It is based on the principle that the attendee wants to know everything there is to know about where he is going and what is in store for him.

You must provide that delegate—via one key mailing—with everything he or she needs to know to get from home, to the meeting site . . . and back again. You must list a complete schedule of events and as much general information about the meeting site as possible. The potential attendee needs, as well, a clear outline of the rules of the game as they apply personally—cost handling, gratuity practices, mode of dress and social program.

You provide all of this information to walk the delegate through the meeting in a colorful advance information release.

This basic advance information release serves as a summary of meeting plans and is sent not only to meeting delegates but to all suppliers of service and senior management as well.

BASIC FORMAT OF THE RELEASE

You can use a duplicating process, printing the release on both sides of colored paper. Transfer letters, clippings, pictures—and a basic theme throughout—make the release an eyecatcher and easy to read.

Attractive, Colorful Cover

The cover should indicate the meeting's name, site and dates—the essential data. If you are incorporating a theme, begin with it here.

Introduction

The introduction should provide the delegate with an enthusiastic description of the present site, along with an outline of previous sites that have been used for the meeting. This historical review brings back pleasant memories, and has the added advantage of letting the hotel people know where you have met before.

The introduction should also include the complete name, address and telephone number of the hotel where the meeting is to be held so that this information can be left with the delegate's home and office.

General Hotel Information

Information about the hotel where delegates will be staying should include: an explanation of registration or pre-registration procedure, early arrival or stayover space availability, the hotel's check-out procedure and time.

Schedule of Events

The release should have a detailed description of what will happen each day. It will include: times and locations for all meals, receptions, business meetings and coffee breaks; scheduled recreational activities and any equipment participants might need; times and locations for any special spouse or children's programs; mode of dress for each event; seating arrangements for dinners; and a list of speakers and topics for business meetings.

Mode of Dress

Most meeting attendees are particularly concerned about the type of clothing they should bring to a meeting, for personal appearance and comfort contribute greatly to enjoyment. You want people to feel "with it."

When supplying mode of dress instructions, determine whether there are any special customs or traditions that apply at the site where you are conducting your meeting. Remember, these customs can vary greatly. Wouldn't it be a shame, for instance, if a guy brought a suit to Acapulco? A suit is perfectly proper for Mexico City—but completely out of order for Acapulco. The attendee would be much more comfortable if he had been able to see something like the following ahead of time:

> A jacket is seldom necessary in Acapulco; a tie, never! The most acceptable outfit day or night is an open-neck sports shirt, slacks and bare feet in sandals. Foot gear should be comfortable—that is the only rule.

For each aspect of your meeting—both business and social—specify the kind of attire that will be appropriate. For instance:

> Attendees at business sessions can dress casually and informally.

Or:

> Dress for Monday evening's steak fry will be casual. Be sure to bring a jacket or sweater if the evening is cool.

Or:

> Wednesday is dress-up night. Formal dress will be in order.

Gear apparel instructions to the expected weather, time of year and general meeting location. For example:

> We can expect spring-like weather during our meeting. Light woolens will be ideal.

Consider the physical structure and layout of the hotel. Is it all under one roof, or does it consist of a series of units that would necessitate people moving in and out of doors to get from one place to another?

Clearly and firmly inform your guests of any hotel requirements regarding dress.

Abbreviated costumes are not allowed in the hotel at any time. Be
sure to bring a cover-up for your bathing suit.

Or:

Whites are required on the tennis court at all times.

General Information

Here you describe climate and weather patterns, available
recreation facilities, points of interest and shopping facilities in the
area, facilities for children and medical services.

If the meeting is being held in a foreign country attendees will
need information regarding customs regulations, language usage and
native customs. You can develop general information packets for
various geographical areas. This eliminates the need for duplicating
the information for every meeting plan; you can simply include the
packet as a supplement with the regular meeting release.

Travel Information

List specific ways and means of traveling to and from the
meeting site—with timetables and destinations.

Hotel Costs

A complete explanation of the rate being paid, applicable tax
and all gratuity arrangements should be included in the release. The
explanation should also include a specific outline of what the
delegate is personally responsible for versus those items for which the
company is paying.

Cost Handling

The delegate should be specifically informed concerning *how*
charges must be paid. Very often you can make arrangements for the
use of personal checks rather than credit cards in order to benefit the
hotel's cash flow.

Questionnaire

This is the most vital part of the advance meeting release as far
as a planner's meeting staff is concerned! The questionnaire is

printed on the last page of the release and the attendee is requested to return it to the office by a certain date.

The questionnaire will outline: whether the invitee will attend; whether his or her spouse will attend; correct spelling of names for badges; intended mode of travel; date and time of arrival and departure; request for early arrival or stay-over space; and participation in scheduled recreational activities.

The bottom part of the questionnaire consists of a pre-registration form to be sent to the hotel. It outlines the attendee's full, formal name, complete home address and firm.

Obviously this walk-through process, including all necessary information in one key mailing, forces the meeting planner to do, in an orderly fashion, all of the basic things that must be done to insure a successful meeting. And now, having apprised the potential attendees of everything they need to know, all communication bases have been touched.

Part Three

THE MEETING: PROGRAM AND STRUCTURE

X

BUSINESS PROGRAMMING

A meeting planner can take an important step toward recognition as a professional by getting more involved in the creation, development and production of conference and convention business programs. Even without specific knowledge of the subject to be presented, a planner can make a positive contribution simply on the basis of having seen—and having been peripherally associated with—a wide variety of business programs.

Too frequently, meeting planners concentrate only on the logistics of the meeting: arranging for sites, equipment, services, entertainment, printing, decorations or transportation. But by giving you these responsibilities it is evident that your organization sees something uncommon in you: you thrive under pressure; you are innovative; you communicate well; you are well-organized; you meet deadlines. And thus you can make many meaningful suggestions regarding the components of a good business program.

The typical business program chairman readily accepts, and even desires, help in structuring the business portion of the meeting. No planner should hesitate to participate in this important segment of an overall successful meeting. In fact, it is *mandatory* if you are to build appreciation for your professional service.

BUSINESS PROGRAM BASICS

Don't schedule serious business programs in the evenings.

Conducting a successful business program requires a lot of common sense. Evening business programs after a long day or a big cocktail party, for instance, are destined for disaster regardless of the subject or the presenter. And a heavy evening business program on a travel day or following a gala dinner is something only the naive or amateur planner allows.

On the other hand, depending on the location and the composition of the audience, a humorous half-hour after-dinner speaker can provide a change of pace as well as some light entertainment. And another alternative is to conduct a crisp 30-minute recognition program between the cocktail party and the actual serving of dinner. Have the orchestra (which is already hired and available) provide back-up music as delegates are presented with plaques; and ask a photographer to be on hand to take pictures.

Six to eight hours a day is the maximum for effective business sessions.

There is a sharp fall-off in the learning retention curve for formal business sessions lasting more than six or eight hours a day. If you *must* formalize business sessions beyond this period, be sure to program in a change of pace such as a long lunch hour or time for recreation in the afternoon.

PROGRAM CONTENT AND STRUCTURE

The opening session is all-important!

Your opening business session is the most important segment of your meeting. If the opening is excellent, it is likely that your whole meeting will be evaluated as "excellent"—even though the other business sessions are only average.

Unfortunately, the converse is also true. If your opening is average, but the rest of the program is outstanding, the meeting will likely be rated "average." Albeit unfair to the total meeting planning effort, this is the way people react. Work hard on your opening business session; and if business program funds are limited, devote a large portion of the budget to the first full day's program.

Speaker Flow

A smooth, interesting transition of speakers and subjects is essential to each business session. *Begin* and *end* with your strongest speakers and/or most important subjects.

If you have five speakers scheduled for a session and two are outstanding, two excellent, and one average, the most effective speaking order is to arrange them so that the first is outstanding, the second excellent, the third average, the fourth excellent—and end with an outstanding speaker to leave the program on an upward note.

Guest speakers should be positioned in the program as early as possible. Delegates then have the opportunity to discuss the subject matter during the remainder of the meeting.

Program Pace

Change of pace is an important consideration in business programming. If, for instance, four speakers and a panel session or motivational film are scheduled, start off with two speakers, follow with the panel or film . . . and wrap up with the last two speakers.

Concurrent Sessions

At times the *general assembly* approach (all delegates attending the same presentation) simply does not meet the diverse needs of the total audience. The answer is concurrent sessions that do. Each individual session, however, must be just as carefully planned and orchestrated as the larger one would have been.

Likewise, discussion groups must be structured to be effective. Leaders with expertise and specific instructions must be placed in each group, or people tend merely to vent themselves with no positive results.

Audience Participation

Developing effective audience participation is no easy task. One simple approach is a random draw which involves challenging each attendee to prepare in advance of the meeting a brief, organized item or sales idea. Draw ten from a hat and devote one hour to these concise presentations.

This type of programming can assure active participation prior to the program as well as during it. Other effective techniques utilize pre-set questions, overhead questions and the "idea machine."

Daily Program Chairman

A program chairman's prime job is to keep the business schedule tied together—and on time! He or she must be as well prepared and rehearsed as each of the presenters; and should be firm and able to use a stop watch effectively. The chairman must be fair to all attendees; and give brief, appropriate introductions.

Moderator

Moderators should not pontificate—and should be given specific instructions not to do so. Their prime job is to keep a discussion group on the assigned subject matter. They should be properly briefed and instructed as to how to draw a response from a group, for "Talkative Terry" and "Reluctant Ralph" need special handling.

Advance Preparation And A-V Coordination

Outlines, speaker schedules, advance scripts, rehearsals incorporating audio-visual support, evaluation of the total program—as much work as possible should be done in advance.

Bear in mind that the proper use of audio-visuals is to provide sound and visual support for a presentation. Audio-visuals should never be used as a crutch. Their purpose is to set the tone and to emphasize important points.

Audience In-Put And Evaluation

Post-meeting evaluation is a must for any professional meeting planning operation. Equally important, however, is a request in advance of the meeting for subject matter which attendees deem to be of critical import. Whether this is done via questionnaire, letter or planning committee, it is essential to get the audience involved *before* the business program is finalized.

XI

BUSINESS PROGRAM FORMAT

Business meetings are either educational, informational or motivational. Often they must answer specific questions and offer solutions to basic industry problems. Accomplishing a meeting's basic business objectives is a difficult task requiring meaningful audience participation. To achieve this goal, the meeting planner must be imaginative and innovative in structuring the business program.

There are a number of basic program formats which have emerged recently and any of them can be adjusted to meet the needs of your company or association and the program you want to present. Each meeting format and set-up, however, must be examined in terms of its applicability and appropriateness for attaining the objectives of this particular meeting. Don't be afraid to experiment, but do so because you honestly believe that the new format might improve audience reception so as to better meet business objectives. Try not to use any one format just because "it has always been done this way" or, conversely, to use a different type of program simply because "everybody else is doing it."

BREAK-OUT SESSIONS

One meeting format which has recently been in vogue is the "rap" session, break-out session or small discussion group. The thought process behind building a rap session into a meeting program seems to be an unchallenged belief in the value of "getting people involved." But just how valid is this thesis that everyone should have an opportunity to express his or her views on any given subject? When applied to a specific educational or motivational goal, it is probably not valid at all!

The cross-pollination of ideas among unproven or average performers—or still worse, among mediocre people of any kind—is a sure way to assure the breeding of mediocrity or, at best, average results. In other words, *what you put in is what you get out.*

Too many planners give too little thought to the planning of their rap session and the general utilization of this meeting tool. They blindly accept the premise that the rap session is good in and of itself and assume that it is a vehicle for stimulating meaningful and worthwhile dialogue . . . and therefore successful meetings. But fall into this trap and before you know it meeting delegates will begin to ask themselves "What did we really accomplish in that session?"

The rap session is by no means an automatic vehicle for successful meetings.

A break-out session or rap session must be well-structured if it is to be worthwhile. This takes hard work, thoughtful research and pre-planning on the part of the meeting planner. Perhaps the following guidelines will be helpful.

Purpose

Define in your own mind what the rap or break-out session should accomplish; what subject matter is to be covered; and what the specific goal is. Be wary of sessions designed merely as a venting exercise for letting off steam. These are as hard to moderate as they are to structure.

In most instances, the purpose of the break-out session will be educational or motivational in nature. If this is the case, the composition of the group requires careful attention as well as a structured set of topics to be discussed.

Composition

Two factors should concern you in planning the composition of a break-out session: leadership and the general make-up of the group.

Moderator

Appoint a moderator *before* the session commences. Don't ask for a volunteer when the session is about to begin. A good moderator should know the subject matter to be discussed, but should also realize that it is not his or her role to give a speech. The moderator should know how to keep the discussion on track—and how to prevent one or two individuals from dominating the scene.

Politics should not be a factor in your choice of a moderator. The Number 1 salesperson in your group may be Number 100 in terms of being a good leader. And if your moderator is conscientious, he or she will make a point of studying the composition of the group prior to the session.

Group Members

Proven leaders who can give meaningful guidance and input to others in the group should blend into the rap session. In positioning high achievers in any of your groups, be sure they are capable of communicating their ideas in an educational and motivational way. Just as your biggest salesman may not prove to be a good moderator, he may not be able to relate to those who are only just beginning. In fact, he may even prove destructive in a group of people who cannot put his advice and guidance into proper perspective. The super achiever might, on the other hand, have an important and beneficial effect on a group of people who are midway up the ladder of success, and this is perhaps the best way to use such a person.

Obviously, the rap or break-out session can be an excellent meeting tool, but it doesn't happen automatically. Work on the purpose and composition of the rap session and it will work for you; take it for granted and you could very well end up with a meeting that is not "worth a rap."

PSYCHOLOGICAL REINFORCEMENT

One of the best tools for assuring full group participation is something I call *Small Group Psychological Reinforcement.* I first heard about it from George Appun in 1975, and have used it in different versions for meetings that range in size from 20 to 400. Here's how it works.

The Audience	Meeting delegates are seated at tables of 6 to 8 people. (Round tables are preferable.) Each table grouping becomes a working team.
Easel, Pad, Crayon	Meeting support items provided for each table.
Recorder-Reporter	Each table group selects one of its members to perform this job.
Program Chairman	Introduces the subject matter to be discussed and the time allotted for each subject.

To illustrate how this format works, let us assume we are attending a meeting planners conference. The participants are seated at twelve round tables for eight; each table is numbered from 1 through 12. Each table has named a Reporter-Recorder (RR).

The program chairman makes a concise statement of the topic to be discussed: *The importance of controlling meeting costs in an inflationary economic environment.* His challenge to the audience is to come up with specific suggestions for controlling or cutting meeting costs within the next 20 minutes.

The RR of each table writes the name of the person contributing an idea and a summary of the basic idea on the easel pad. It is very important for the RR to write the name of the contributor on the pad. Doing this serves as a positive stimulator for all group members to participate. Each person wants to get his or her name on the pad. And believe me, this simple technique works.

After the allocated time for discussion has passed, the program chairman calls on three or four RRs to share a full report of their group's findings or suggestions with the general audience. It is vital that the chairman ask for three or four full reports.

Inevitably many of the ideas or solutions are the same—by repetition they become indelibly imprinted in the minds of the audience as practical things to do—thus psychologically reinforcing their importance and adaptability. The program chairman, if he so elects, can next ask the RRs who were not called upon to give a full report, if their groups came up with any additional points thus far not covered. Often this results in additional input.

Watching this meeting format in action, you can see some subtle, positive things begin to happen. Most noticeable is that the table groups compete among themselves to come up with the most or best ideas. Within the groups, because of their small size and the name recording technique, even the shy person contributes.

The possible variations of the format are too numerous to outline fully. Obviously, at a small meeting of three to four table groupings, each RR is asked to give a full report. At a large meeting with several table groupings, a bowl drawing of three or four table numbers randomly selected is a good technique for determining who will be asked to give a full report. The RR assignment can be rotated; this keeps everybody alert. A separate program chairman can be used to introduce each subject to be discussed.

You can go on and on with variations of the basic technique. The main thing is that it works and that it functions as an excellent agent for action and as a vehicle for getting specific solutions to problems as well as answers to key questions.

THE IDEA MACHINE

This program format of "The Idea Machine" is particularly useful because of its simplicity and adaptability to groups of all sizes—as well as the ease with which variations in format can be implemented.

Scorers

Three people from the audience are nominated to be "scorers." They are given flash number cards—running from 1 to 10—usually 8½ by 11 inches in size.

Recorder

One person is elected to record the scores posted by the "scorers." He records the name of the "idea presenter," the subject matter, and the number of points. In a small group, this information could be put on an easel pad.

Moderator

The moderator introduces the subject matter to be discussed . . . indicates whom from the audience shall speak . . . and controls the long-winded speaker.

Let us assume, again, that we are at another meeting planners conference. The moderator announces the first subject to be discussed: *Successful Meeting Promotion Ideas.*

Joe Brown

Suggests that the mayor of the city in which the meeting is being held send a letter of welcome to each delegate. Scorers rate his idea 6 - 6 - 7, for a total of 19 points.

Bill Green

Suggests that a colored brochure, de-

picting the highlights of the meeting site,
be sent to each delegate. Scorers rate
his idea 3 - 3 - 4, for a total of 10 points.

The Recorder   Records the name of the person sug-
gesting the idea, the gist of his sugges-
tion and his point total.

This procedure continues until all ideas have been exhausted or the
time allocated for this particular subject has been used up. If you
wish, the person accumulating the most points for his idea might be
given a small prize—or special recognition such as a distinctive
badge ribbon.

Other Versions

You can readily see how "The Idea Machine" can be adapted to
meeting groups of all kinds. If, for example, the group consists of
insurance salespersons, proposed subjects might be "prospecting,"
"closing techniques" or "power phrases." If the group is made up of
accountants, a proposed subject might be "tax saving ideas for the
small businessman."

There are also many variations you can try to sharpen this
meeting tool for your purposes:

1. Let your delegates know what the subject matter to be discussed
via the "Idea Machine" is going to be in advance. This gives them a
chance to do some advance thinking.

2. Set various time limits for each proposed subject—5, 10, 15, 20
minutes, depending on the importance of the subject to be discussed.

3. After each subject, or after each second or third subject, change
the moderator, scorers and recorder. This gives a change of pace to
your meeting and assures more constructive audience participation
by involving more people.

4. Recognize ideas. Whether you use prizes, ribbons, or a listing of winners in next year's business program, be sure to have the business program chairman for the day thank each person for presenting an idea. Even if a particular idea does not receive many points, it is meaningful if it is new and helpful to one delegate. "Thanks to all" is truly in order after this type of session.

5. For large audiences, the basic idea still applies; however, you may want to use a vu-graph and screen for scoring and recording. Also, hand microphones on long cords, which can be moved throughout the audience, would be helpful in a large group.

XII

GUEST
SPEAKERS

Behind every guest speaker is a program chairman praying for success. But while prayers may be helpful, the adoption of a professional approach to the selection and hiring of guest speakers is a far surer guarantee of an effective outcome. Over the years I have hired speakers ranging from Erma Bombeck, Harry Reasoner, Martin Agronsky, Larry Wilson, Bill Gove and John Richters to unknowns who sell cemetery plots. One thing I've learned is essential:

> **Regardless of how good or renowned a guest speaker is, he or she will not be fully successful if the presentation does not fit into into the overall purpose of the meeting.**

The decision to bring in an outside speaker is a major one. Once that decision is made, the hard task begins—selecting the *right* speaker. To insure maximum return on the investment of dollars and program time, that selection should be based on *professional* objectives, criteria and research.

WHY HAVE A GUEST SPEAKER?

By examining the reasons for bringing in an outside speaker, a meeting planner establishes his or her objectives and narrows the field of prospects. The major reasons for employing speakers are: 1) to educate; 2) to entertain; or 3) to impress the audience. The first step, therefore, in hiring a speaker is to realize which of these ends is to be accomplished.

A speaker should not be selected who does not satisfy at least one—hopefully more—of the above criteria. But it is often possible to find a speaker who, for example, is prestigious as well as amusing; or highly informative as well as renowned. Beware, at all costs, of the "professional" speaker with no other area of expertise. The best speakers do not make their living solely as speakers; and canned motivational messages can have a deadly effect, particularly on today's sophisticated audiences.

FINDING AND SELECTING
GUEST SPEAKERS

Hard as it may be for struggling young speaking candidates to believe, finding the right guest speaker to fit a business program's purpose and objective can be a difficult, time consuming and frustrating task. Ideally, to ascertain a speaker's appropriateness, it is best to attend a sample presentation to judge delivery and message.

In lieu of such an opportunity, a planner can maintain files of brochures and advertisements mailed by various speakers and their agents. Seldom, however, do I depend on these to select a guest speaker, for the following sources have proven most successful.

Other Speakers And Speakers Bureaus

Speakers you have used previously know you and your organization. Through professional groups, like the *National Speakers Association,* speakers are getting to know one another better and their recommendations are generally excellent. In addition, there are several good professional bureaus—notably the National Speakers Bureau and the American Program Bureau—which recommend speakers whom they represent.

Other Meeting Planners

Meeting planners across the country are establishing contact through organizations such as *Meeting Planners International* and the *Insurance Conference Planners Association.* One of the benefits of membership in such an organization is the opportunity to gain and share information on speakers and how they can contribute to a program.

Business Associates

If you are associated with a large company you know people of diverse talents and interests. Many of them will have excellent suggestions which reflect not only their job responsibilities but their personal interests as well.

Editors And Publishers Of Trade Magazines

Magazines such as *Meetings & Conventions, Successful Meetings, Meeting News* and the *Insurance Conference Planner* are generally excellent, objective sources. By the nature of their work, editors and publishers of these magazines travel a great deal, attend many meetings—and hear many speakers.

Regardless of the source of recommendations, always request and check a speaker's references. Interview the prospective speaker and make your goals and expectations clear.

Once the decision to hire has been made, speaker and planner have certain responsibilities to one another. They are as follows:

GUEST SPEAKER'S RESPONSIBILITIES

1. To arrive on time, well-prepared and sober, ready to provide all services agreed to.
2. To provide biographical information, photos, etc. in a timely and orderly manner.
3. To inform the planner, well in advance of the meeting, of any special introduction that is needed.
4. To advise the planner, at the time of accepting the booking, of special meeting room and presentation support items necessary.
5. To advise the planner, well in advance of the meeting, of travel plans to and from the meeting site; and to request special assistance with these plans as needed.
6. To cover agreed-upon subject matter.
7. Never to speak down to an audience.
8. Never to use profanity or off-color jokes.
9. Never to incorporate a name of a member of the audience without first clearing its use and pronunciation with the meeting planner.
10. To seek approval, prior to accepting the booking, to sell tapes, books or similar items.
11. To begin and end the presentation within the agreed-upon time format.
12. To place as few demands as possible on the meeting planner during the meeting. (All points of coordination should be handled before the meeting.)

MEETING PLANNER'S RESPONSIBILITIES

1. To present the quest speaker with a clearly written outline of what is expected, including the following items:
   a. Arrival and departure dates and times. If possible, insist that the speaker arrive the day before the scheduled presentation, in time to participate in the evening's social/business activities. The speaker then gets a feel for his audience and is

rested the next day. The planner's anxiety about on-time arrival is also eliminated.
   b. Subject matter to be presented.
   c. Presentation format and timing.
2. To present the speaker with a written agreement concerning business arrangements and expense reimbursements, including the following:
   a. Honorarium or fee, and any advance required for travel or meeting-related expenses.
   b. Out of pocket expenses covered; billing procedure and invoice statements required.
   c. Authorized mode of travel (tourist or first class) and departure and destination points.
   d. Spouse invitation (whether and at whose expense).
   e. Written permission for use of speaker's photograph and biographical information other than for listing in the program; autographs; and taping and distribution of cassette copies of the presentation.
3. To provide an audience profile, including the following information:
   a. Purpose and objective of the meeting and prime purpose of hiring the speaker.
        Is the meeting an educational seminar or a recognition or incentive program? What is the speaker expected to accomplish?
   b. An overview of the total business program.
        Emphasize topics and speakers immediately preceding and following the speaker to assist him in making a relaxed and personalized presentation without duplication.
   c. Background information on sponsoring organization.
        Annual reports are ideal. The speaker should know if the organization is coming off a good or a bad year.
        Proper pronunciation of the name of the organization and the specific name of the meeting should be stressed to avoid embarrassing mistakes.
   d. Names and titles of VIPs in the audience.

e.   Composition of the audience.

   Male or female? Delegates and spouses? Home office or
   field? Management or sales personnel? Age distribution?
   Income level? Educational level? Liberal or conserva-
   tive? Expected response to planned subject matter.

4. To treat the guest as a VIP.

   Every effort should be made to make the speaker feel good
   about being a part of the program.

   Pre-register him at the hotel and assign a top-quality
   room. Flowers or some appropriate gift should be placed
   in the room—especially if spouse is attending.

   At registration desk leave a handwritten note of welcome and reconfirm time and place of meeting and scheduled presentation.

5. To provide assistance with arrival and departure.

   Most speakers prefer not to be met at the airport and with
   proper travel information, can get to the meeting site on their
   own. They should, however, be given the option of being met.
   Moreover, with speakers of great importance you may want
   to simply state that they will be met—and by whom.

   At departure time alert the hotel desk so that appropriate
   charges are automatically transferred to master account.
   (Any personal charges can be posted on the speaker's bill and
   simply deducted from the speaking fee. The speaker need
   only leave his key at the desk.

SCHEDULING
THE GUEST SPEAKER

A typical meeting runs for three nights and three full days. The
principal guest speaker is frequently scheduled for the last day—
though often for no better reason than "We've always done it this
way" or the belief that such placement boosts the last day's
attendance. The results of such logic are more myth than reality.
Good guest speakers are expensive; and they should be utilized to get

the maximum return on the dollars and program time expended.

Schedule the guest speaker as early in the meeting program as possible—not on the last day.

The rationale behind this recommendation is simple: Having hired a speaker with unique viewpoints and ideas that relate to your overall program, you should give the delegates an opportunity to discuss those ideas. If the guest speaker is scheduled for the last day, delegates are departing, rendering such discussion impossible.

Don't schedule another speaker immediately following the guest speaker.

If selection has been done properly, you have hired an outstanding speaker, and it is not fair to a typical in-house amateur, regardless of how good or well-prepared, to have to follow a professional.

A good guest speaker, well-informed and selected with the meeting's objective in mind, will be a positive contribution to the meeting.

Part Four

**DURING THE MEETING:
FOOD, BEVERAGE AND
ENTERTAINMENT**

XIII

FIRST TIMERS

Attending one's first meeting can be a traumatic experience . . .

Will anyone know me? Sure I qualified, but I was lucky; I'm hardly one of the big hitters . . . I wish I could have bought a new suit . . .

Or what about the spouse?

Gosh, the babysitter is expensive . . . Maybe I shouldn't go . . . after all, what will I do? I hope I did the right thing, blowing the budget on that dress . . . What if it's too fancy? . . . What will they think of me? . . . I won't know anyone!

These fears of the unknown are very real for people coming to their first meeting. Even the seasoned attendee often experiences first-day jitters.

Never is a meeting planner in a more commanding or potentially helpful position than on check-in day. For by being a good professional planner—organized, disciplined and having put a lot of time into the advance planning of this meeting—the planner can turn what might have been a traumatic experience for new meeting-goers into a delightful one.

Earn your prestige as a professional and your rapport with

meeting delegates, particularly first-timers, by employing the following devices:

Meeting Registration and Greeting Area

At all major meetings, particularly those which will be attended by spouses, a meeting registration and greeting area should be set up. Here meeting kits containing badges, guest lists, updated programs, dinner invitations and other helpful items of information can be handed out. In particular, this is the place to issue a warm greeting or to offer assistance. Be quick to introduce yourself; say "Hi!" and "Welcome!"

Although other corporate or association executives and senior delegates may be on hand to assist with this activity, it is most important for the meeting planner to be there during the entire hotel and meeting registration process. You want to be readily accessible to give *any* delegate *any* help that will make him or her feel more at ease. You want to be able to relieve any concerns or solve any problems *on the spot*—before they develop into a major irritant.

Check-In Day Hospitality Center

As close as possible to the meeting registration area—adjacent to it, if it is at all practical or permissable—establish a hospitality center where coffee, soft drinks and sandwiches or snacks are served. This is a place where people are made to feel welcome, a place where they can ask questions, a place to relax, renew friendships . . . and make new ones. Above all, it is a place where delegates will feel that someone—*their* meeting planner—is looking after them.

Distinctive First-Time Name Badges

A special name badge for first-timers is a way of letting the other delegates know that people are first-timers. Seasoned delegates and executives, knowing this, can then greet them warmly and give them special consideration.

Special Reception For First-Timers

About a half an hour before the first evening's general reception, schedule a separate early reception for first-timers. Ideally, it should be in a separate location to insure privacy and a relaxed, intimate atmosphere for getting to know one another. Senior executives should host this activity, for it is often the only time when they can be sure of meeting the new people. Following the special reception, first-timers then attend the general reception—knowing at least each other.

Dinner Seating

For the first evening's dinner, assign all attendees table seatings by individual invitation. First-timers come to the meeting looking forward to meeting some of the top brass or super salepersons. They can be assured of meeting them if they are dining with them, so control the seating arrangements with a mixture of first-timers and VIPs at each table.

The Buddy System

This takes a little paper work, but it gets a lot of people involved and is well worth the effort. Here's how it works . . .

In advance of the meeting, a letter goes out from headquarters to a senior representative, someone who's been coming to meetings for a long time, introducing a first-time qualifier. Tell a little about the new person—spouse, children, school, accomplishments, etc.

Ask the senior person to write to the new qualifier, congratulating him or her and offering to be of assistance during the upcoming meeting. The senior is not expected to babysit for the new person, but just to let him or her know in advance that they are welcome and that a high achiever is looking forward to their meeting. This program pays great dividends and costs very little—just some time and a couple of stamps.

Recognition Programs

First-timer qualifiers, as well as other deserving delegates, can be part of the special recognition program at, say, the first day's general assembly business session. Bring them forward with a flourish and in the spirit of good fun. Present them with a special memento—a charm, a photograph or a plaque—to show your company's or association's appreciation.

Go out of your way to make all delegates feel wanted, needed and warmly welcome at your meetings with special breakfasts, business sessions and enjoyable ceremonies. This goes for old-timers as well as first-timers.

With care and advanced planning, these events will be a delightful experience for all concerned—but especially for the first time attendee. One never forgets his or her first meeting; and you have the power to make it a pleasant memory.

XIV

COCKTAIL PARTIES AND RECEPTIONS

The cocktail party or reception is an important meeting event which can be used to accomplish many objectives. Generally speaking, a cocktail party is the most obvious vehicle for social/business exchange. More particularly, it may be used to recognize award winners or to introduce important persons. In any case, cocktail parties and receptions represent a significant portion of the meeting's financial investment. And if they are to accomplish any objective worthy of the investment, careful attention must be paid to the planning details—*on the scene as well as behind it.*

Basic planning errors—those that a meeting attendee might readily observe—occur when the meeting planner overlooks the basics such as traffic flow, lighting, decoration, background music and levels of service staff.

Frequently, a planner assumes that since the hotel or restaurant has conducted so many cocktail parties in the past, this one will take care of itself. This is a big mistake! Seldom will the hotel's standards meet the stringent ones of the professional meeting planner. And even if by some chance they do, the amateur will probably pay more than necessary. In the worst case, neither the meeting planner nor the hotel has the time and/or specific knowledge to plan adequately.

PURPOSE OF THE PARTY

The first question to answer when planning a reception or cocktail party is: **What is the purpose of the party?**

The physical arrangements—location, size and type of food and refreshments served, for example—will vary according to the party's purpose or the objective it is aimed to accomplish. Whether we are saying "thanks" or just providing a brief interlude for fellowship, a cocktail party is basically designed so that people can meet and have contact with one another.

Now, let us illustrate some of the ways cocktail parties can be used to enhance our meetings.

A Recognition Vehicle For First Time Attendees

At qualifying agent meetings, for instance, the opening evening's first social/business activity might commence with a 30-45 minute "First Timers Reception" preceding the reception for all delegates. This reception is preferably conducted in a separate but nearby location.

The purpose of the smaller, more intimate gathering is to give the first-time qualifiers an opportunity to meet each other, corporate officials and top field achievers they might not get to meet during the larger general reception.

The association executive can utilize the same concept by conducting an opening reception for first-time meeting registrants and spouses. Once again, they get a chance to meet each other, the president of the association, members of the board of directors and other prominent members of the association. Having met these important people, they begin to feel more like "part of the group."

To Recognize Longevity, Sustained Achievement Or Special Accomplishment

Using a cocktail party as a recognition tool is another way of supporting the management concept that *you get what you reward*. Salute the people who are the backbone of your organization or who have provided unusual support with a special reception in their honor.

Old-timers frequently feel that they are forgotten when meeting time comes along. For them, take an approach which is similar to that just described for first-timers.

At special recognition receptions, a receiving line is a charming old-fashioned nicety that assures everyone's introduction. And if spouses are invited, consider presenting them (the female ones, that is) with a corsage. Wristlets which come along with a large pin permit the recipient to wear the corsage either on her wrist or on her clothing.

A Gathering Point

As meeting planners, we are often moving people from one location to another. Rather than instruct your people to simply assemble in the lobby, a more impressive approach, if the budget permits, is to conduct a short reception at the appointed gathering point. Serve punch or a glass of wine if cost is a major stumbling block. If it seems appropriate for what you have planned for the evening, make provisions for a "roader," a drink in a plastic or paper cup. Such an extra would be nice, for instance, on the way to a western cook-out.

PHYSICAL PLANNING

Traffic Flow

Good traffic flow—or its absence—is the first, most readily observable aspect of cocktail party planning. Your delegates want to move around and meet others. Pick a location that permits this kind of circulation. *Don't squeeze people in!*

Make sure that bar stations and hors d'oeuvre tables are not placed near entrances; rather, locate them so that they draw people in to the room. Spread bar stations out to eliminate congestion—and never place bars near hors d'oeuvre tables. If your group is very large, place a number of small hors d'oeuvre tables in different areas or combine placement with waiters or waitresses passing hors d'oeuvres.

Bar Stations

One bar station per 100 guests is a good minimum standard. If you go slightly over 100 guests, say by 10 or 20 people, two bar stations should be used. If two bar stations are employed, they should not be used in double format. Separate distribution points allow a better flow of people.

Hotels and restaurants do not like this approach because two separate service set-ups must be made for glasses, mixes, garnishes, etc.; the meeting planner, however, should insist upon it.

Waiter/Waitress Service

At VIP affairs, large gatherings or receptions that include spouses or a large number of females, supplement bar station distribution with waiter/waitress service. This is not only a nicety, but a work procedure which can greatly improve the speed of service.

You might also want to have your guests met as they enter the reception area by waiters and waitresses carrying trays of the most popular drinks. Drinks served in this fashion could be color-coded to identify different varieties—red swizzle sticks for scotch and soda, blue for bourbon and water, green for gin and tonic. Of course, waiters or waitresses can take individual orders if the tray approach does not appeal to you and delegates want different types of drinks.

If you do use the latter type of service, make absolutely sure there are provisions for a private, screened-off service bar. Many guests, both male and female, prefer to walk up to a bar and order their own drink; and nothing irritates this guest more than being stuck behind a waiter or waitress placing a large order. It is worth the extra bartender charge to eliminate this potential hazard before it occurs by establishing a separate service location.

Lighting

Bright lights and glare are distractions that can be easily eliminated. Adjust the lighting to create the atmosphere you desire. Remember, however, that name badges must be easy to read at all times in all locations. It is no fun to attend a cocktail party in the dark, so beware of this sure sign of poor planning.

If conducting a party out of doors, try to do so during daylight hours. If this is not feasible, be sure to make arrangements for adequate artificial lighting.

Music

Use live music to support your basic reason for getting together. Do not let it become a distraction.

I do not recommend entertainment at a cocktail party for the simple reason that the prime purpose of most such receptions is to stimulate people into getting to know one another. If you make your party a three-ring circus, you have built in conflicting purposes.

On the other hand, music, appropriately used can be a big plus. A violin to invite people into the reception area, for instance, is a nice touch. Or soft background music can set the tone of the reception and relax participants. But never let it become the dominating feature of the reception.

Decorations

A small additional expense often makes a big difference when it comes to enhancing the decor for your party. Don't go overboard; but the imaginative use of ferns or colored lighting can have a soft but substantial impact on the atmosphere of a reception. Likewise, simple decorations, like flowers and wine bottle displays have great eye appeal . . . and show the attendees, quite simply, that you care.

Ash Trays

Smoking is becoming less and less fashionable—and more and more irritating to the non-smoker; but for the benefit of all, provide for prompt removal of offensive, smouldering cigarettes. Be sure you have ash trays—and that they are kept clean!

Seating Arrangements

Some guests will inevitably arrive either disabled or extremely tired after a long day of business sessions or traveling. Make sure, therefore, that there is at least a sprinkling of seats at each reception you conduct.

Increase the number of seats each successive day of the meeting. Stand-up cocktail parties three or four consecutive evenings can be an arduous task for older delegates; and if you have a series of such parties on the program, plan on being able to seat 20-25% of the expected guests.

Weather

Weather can play havoc with the best of plans. So, if an outdoor party is planned, an alternate location indoors should also be booked.

Equally important is a previously designated *decision time* when you and the hotel management must decide *go* or *no go*. The meeting planner instinctively wants to make this decision as late as possible, while the supplier of service will want an early decision. You will eliminate this potential harassment by deciding, during your advance planning session, *when* the decision will be made.

Closing The Cocktail Hour

Bringing a cocktail party—especially a successful one—to a close is no easy task. Everyone seems to want to have that one last drink; and neither flashing lights nor whistles nor gongs are very effective.

The best solution is to simply shut down bar service at the designated hour—with the announcement by waiters, waitresses, captains and yourself that "dinner is being served." Then, set a good example by getting to dinner on time yourself and bringing another couple or group with you. This should start the movement into the dining room; and if seating arrangements have been clearly indicated in advance, people will find their places easily and the meal can proceed on schedule.

HORS D'OEUVRES

With the high prices of food today, hors d'oeuvre selection has assumed increased importance in cocktail party and reception planning. Be very careful, and you will waste neither food nor money. Consider your hors d'oeuvre planning successful if you begin to run out of food shortly before dinner.

Buying Guidelines

If buying on a *piece basis,* use a planning figure of five per person.

When buying hot or cold hors d'oeuvres on a *per person basis,* use a stipulated preparation count of approximately three fourths of expected attendance. To simplify accounting, give a specific number rather than a percentage figure. If I expected 400 guests, for example, I would ask for a *per person* preparation count of 300. Thus, if the agreed upon price was $5 per person, the follow-up accounting review is simple—300 × $5 plus applicable tax and gratuities.

Rationale For Hors d'Oeuvres

There are two basic reasons for serving hors d'oeuvres:

1. To bridge appetites between meals; and
2. To temper the effects of alcohol.

Meeting or convention evening meals are usually scheduled between 7:30 and 8:15 p.m. Depending upon the area of the country from which the individual delegate comes—and his or her work habits—the typical American meeting attendee eats dinner at home between 5:30 and 6:30 p.m. Hors d'oeuvres thus play an important role in your reception planning by bridging appetites between meals and tempering the effects of alcohol.

One mistake the meeting planner should not make is to neglect to coordinate the hors d'oeuvre selection with the planned evening meal. This can be disastrous in terms of poorly spent dollars as well as wasted food.

Hors d'Oeuvre Selection

The hors d'oeuvre selection should not blunt appetities. The morale of the kitchen staff behind the scene can easily be destroyed if platter after platter of beautifully prepared food returns only partially eaten. This could have a negative impact on meal preparation and service for the remainder of your meeting.

The golden rule is to balance hors d'oeuvre selection with the basic dinner entree to be served. If a light evening meal is planned, like fish or poultry, heavier, more expensive hors d'oeuvres are appropriate. Otherwise, keep to light, simple eye-appealing selections. If a heavy deluxe meal, like prime rib or Beef Wellington, is planned, serve, for example, simple canapes or dry snacks supplemented with cheese spreads. Cold vegetables with dips would also be appropriate. The latter are inexpensive and well-received by most meeting attendees, and they are attractive as well as low in calories.

Eye appeal does play a role in the selection of hors d'oeuvres. Cold canapes, attractively trayed and color-coordinated, are a real art. Some meeting planners, however, order fancy hors d'oeuvres merely to impress their attendees; and in today's world of escalating costs, this is an unwarranted extravagance.

DRINKS

There are times when you want to strictly limit the choice of drinks at a reception or party—and serve, for instance, only wine or beer. Under these conditions service is much simpler, and the budget can be closely guarded. But naturally, for a standard cocktail party you will want to have on hand all of the different types of drinks your group might request. You should always think about including the following.

Soft Drinks And Beer

Some delegates are beer drinkers. Some don't drink at all. Make sure that beer and soft drinks are available—and that some of the latter are of the diet variety.

Wine

Regardless of how small your group is, as a bare minimum have a choice of red or white wine at your bar station. It is a must! And an attractive wine table with select choices can be the centerpiece of your reception.

Exotic Drinks

The expense involved may prohibit this type of service, but an exotic drink station serving tropical delights or liqueurs—or Irish Coffee or coffee and Kahlua—can make a tremendous hit.

Punch

A fancy punch bowl and sparkling, attractive punch adds a touch of class and frequently reduces overall costs by cutting down on regular bar service.

Local Color

When in Rome do as the Romans do. Serve drinks that are typical of the area in which you are holding your meeting. A professionally planned party will always serve drinks which are appropriate to the time and locale—hot mulled cider in the fall in New England . . . Yellow Birds in the Caribbean . . . Mint Juleps in the traditional South.

Special Requests

Every now and again there is a group or an important person who drinks only one unusual thing. Maybe the chairman of the board drinks only sherry. If you want to keep these people happy, and you know about their idiosyncrasy, make special arrangements to have their favorite on hand.

NEGOTIATING THE PARTY

Negotiating and organizing a party or reception can be a lot of fun for the meeting planner. Many things must be considered and

many decisions made that the meeting delegate will never be aware
of. But to do your job properly you must take the time to evaluate
alternate ways to "buy" your party.

How do you buy liquor? There is no simple answer, for the "right
way" will vary from location to location and from group to group.

Buying Liquor—Per Drink vs. Per Bottle

When evaluating a *per drink* price quote, ask the obvious
question—What size drink do you serve? Drinks will vary from one
ounce to an ounce and three quarters. The best alternative is a 1¼
ounce drink. The per drink price is relatively straightforward—so
much per 1¼ ounce drink.

**Stipulate that drinks be measured via a jigger or
automatic dispenser. Never permit free pouring or
you will end up with a very intoxicated group.**

Freepouring is particularly probable if you are buying liquor
by the bottle, so that is another consideration. In addition,
evaluating a *per bottle* price is a little more complicated. There are
26 ounces in a fifth, 32 ounces in a quart. Plan on 20 drinks per fifth,
24 to 25 per quart. An allowance must be made for spillage; and
when evaluating a *per bottle* quote, make sure prices include mixes
and bar set-ups.

If buying by the bottle, be sure to ascertain how "partials,"
opened but not empty bottles, are to be handled. Does the hotel or
restaurant render credit on partials or are you stuck with them at the
end of the party? If partials cannot be returned for credit, you will be
just amazed at how many bottles get opened during the last ten
minutes of a party. If credit is not rendered on partial bottles, give
very serious consideration to discarding this alternative and buying
by the drink.

The next step is to evaluate the price of what is being served.
House brands or standard bar stock will vary from location to
location. At some facilities V.O. and J & B Scotch will routinely be
part of the regular bar stock. At another facility, these same brands

may be classified as *premium* or *call brands* and subject to an extra charge. Determine *what* you are buying and for *how much*.

All special arrangements and agreements should be obtained in writing.

Package Price Cocktail Parties—Including Hors d'Oeuvres

Some hotels offer a complete party package for one price. Assuming that brands of liquor and service standards are met, this is very attractive from an accounting viewpoint, for you will know exactly how much you are going to spend per person.

However, you had better know your group very well before entering into such an arrangement. Built into such packaging are the hotel's assumed consumption standards. Nevertheless, while a group comprised of men and women will generally consume three drinks per person per hour, an all male group will drink three and a half to four drinks per hour.

If you know your group is a late arriving one, make absolutely sure that a factor for time breakage is built in—say, an extension of the cocktail hour by ten minutes at your discretion with no extra charge. Otherwise, "time over" is on a straight pro rata basis and this can become very expensive.

Cash Bars vs. Sponsored Bars

Bear in mind the simple truth—**People drink more when somebody else is paying for it!** Cash bars also require more staff and ticket sellers. So when negotiating the price for a party you are sponsoring, make sure that your agreed upon price is *less* than cash bar prices.

STAFFING THE PARTY

Bartenders

Price per drink and size of drink don't mean much by themselves. You must also ascertain and study what service levels are built into the price. Generally, the price is based on a bar station, bartender and bar boy. Be sure you know how many separate bar stations are planned, their location and staff complement.

Bartender Charges

A *bartender charge* is usually a house charge. The money goes to the hotel or restaurant, not the bartender. In most instances this charge can be eliminated if consumption is high enough and some minimum amount of liquor is dispensed. The specific amount will vary from one facility to another.

Negotiate in advance the consumption required to offset a bartender charge. This consumption figure may range anywhere from $100 to $300 worth of liquor per hour. If you cannot negotiate this charge, be sure to include it when evaluating your *per drink* price quote.

Waiter/Waitress Service

Is waiter or waitress service included in your price quote? If not, try to negotiate this service—based on anticipated consumption—into your deal.

House Or Union Work Rules

As a general rule, a waiter or waitress who is called in to serve a luncheon must be paid for a minimum of two or three hours. To serve a dinner they must be paid for three to four hours. As these standards of payment will vary from one location to another, always inquire as to what the hourly work rule payment will be.

Usually, if you are having a dinner at the same location as the cocktail party, the waiter or waitress service can be had at no additional cost during the reception. The service people are being paid anyway. The only additional charge you will incur is for additional service bar set-up.

If this is true, why isn't such service made standard by hotel and restaurant operations? Primarily because bartenders don't like it, for the more help servicing the party, the greater the number of people splitting the gratuity pie.

Most cocktail party prices—when a dinner is not involved—do

not include waiter or waitress service. Prices are normally based on a bar station service set-up; and under these circumstances (no dinner involved) you can anticipate a charge that will range from $10 to $25 per waiter/waitress. This is often a negotiable item that can be recovered if consumption is high enough—but under no circumstances will it be removed if you neglect to discuss it ahead of time.

COST CONTROL AND BAR AUDITING

Know Your Group

Numerous war stories are told of bartenders pouring bottles of liquor down the sink, excessive spillage and poor auditing of hotel liquor control points—hence inflated and inaccurate liquor bills. Meeting planners, in retaliation, have devised complex techniques like bottle stamping or personal review of each bottle.

Early in my career I worked in a similar manner but soon found I had neither the staff nor the personal time to devote to this aspect of meeting management. I did, however, have good records of past consumption at other locations—as well as common sense. Having observed the drinking patterns of my meeting delegates, I now regularly and accurately predict the liquor consumption for each evening of a meeting.

Some groups tend to have a big first night and taper off after that. Other groups, generally management types, tend to drink more the second evening of a meeting. So . . .

> **Past records, including the length of time bars are left open, are a vitally important and excellent form of cost control.**

Budget Bar

Another common cost control, and a relatively easy one for the meeting planner to implement, is a budget bar based on a maximum consumption figure. To illustrate its application, let us assume we have a group of 300 people for cocktails. We assume the average drink per person is $1.50; and we assume slightly more than three drinks per person during the party—or $5 per person for liquor. We simply instruct the hotel, that once $1,500 worth (300 × $5) of beverages has been served, further liquor service must be approved by the meeting planner. If this happens in fifteen minutes, something is wrong. If it happens five minutes before the scheduled closing hours, you have a simple decision to make—to continue serving or to close the bar early. At this stage of the game, you at least have some idea of what the overall costs are going to be.

Many other ideas of ways to control costs could be offered, but estimates based on past experience, common sense or a previously budgeted and set amount have proved to be most successful for me.

What If The Bill Is Too High?

When it comes to the billing for a large cocktail party or reception, a multitude of human errors are possible—anything from a simple mistake in addition to paying for someone else's party. Often the problem is easily solved. What seems like an inordinately high bill may be offset by a large stock of partially used bottles, the contents of which may be used at your next affair. Or, if you have made such an arrangement in advance, they might be calculated for credit on your present bill.

To begin with, when working towards a solution of such a problem it is best to keep the discussion on as low a management level as possible, preferably with the food and beverage or banquet manager. Simply state that based on your knowledge of the group involved you feel that the bill is too high and that you would like to see—*please*—a review of how the charges were determined. If you find any errors, ask them to resubmit—again, *please*—a corrected bill.

If the above approach does not immediately receive a satisfactory explanation and/or solution, get the hotel's general manager or sales manager involved. Food and beverage directors don't like their kingdoms invaded, and this step is seldom necessary. Remember that your first responsibility as a meeting planner is the proper representation of your company or association. Don't hesitate to take whatever

COCKTAIL PARTIES AND RECEPTIONS

steps are necessary if you genuinely feel that you have been "put on." The best way to earn respect is to raise questions at the right time— when something can still be easily done about the problem and everything is still fresh in everyone's mind.

XV

WINE

Changing lifestyles and tastes are clearly reflected in today's typical meeting delegate's attitude toward wine. During the fifties and early sixties wine served at meals was considered to be a real highlight. But today's cuisine and calorie conscious delegate is far more sophisticated. For many, wine is now an intimate part of everyday life; and it is a regular part of the menu rather than a luxury. The meeting planner who recognizes this trend can fulfill delegates' expectations—and accomplish many other objectives at the same time.

A VINTAGE AFFAIR

Wine can be utilized to enhance a meeting in any number of ways, limited only by the extent of a planner's ingenuity and adventurous inclination. Wine can be both less expensive and more elegant than regular liquor service. And one more thing to bear in mind: the traditional guidelines—white wine with fish or fowl, red wine with red meat—no longer apply. Now almost anything goes, so let us look at some of the most effective ways to serve wine.

Wine At A Sponsored Reception

Any meeting planner worth his or her grapes should incorporate a wine table (with selected cheeses, if desired) as an integral part of the cocktail party/reception plan. By so doing, the following objectives are accomplished:

1. Meeting the needs and desires of an increasing number of delegates.

2. Providing a vehicle which, properly selected, can significantly reduce total reception costs. Moderately priced wines on a *per glass* basis will always cost less than a standard cocktail. And a table of wine accompanied by cheeses permits buying a smaller quantity of high priced hot and cold hors d'oeuvres.

3. Wine tables—with a few fancy ice containers, circular bottle displays, perhaps a few flowers—can, at little or no cost, be an appealing addition to a reception.

Wine With Dinner

A choice of red or white wine should be incorporated into the service for all sponsored meals, parties and receptions. The basic reason for this is that it is both hospitable and economical. As evidence I give you the following:

1. All delegates are made to feel properly hosted—because *all* tables, not just a select few, are the recipients of wine during dinner.

2. By instructing hotel management personnel to have waiters ask whether red or white wine is desired as soon as a delegate is seated you eliminate the well known cocktail party withdrawal symptoms. This action eliminates the rash of individual liquor orders which can so negatively disrupt dinner service.

3. At the same time you are improving dinner service, you are eliminating expensive individual liquor and wine ordering.

Rules For Wine Service

1. White wines and rosé wines should be served chilled; reds at room temperature.

2. Ice should never be put in the glasses. It dilutes the wine, enfeebling its character.

3. Wine glasses are normally 6 to 8 ounces in size. If possible, instruct the hotel to use the smaller size glass.

4. Insist on *two* wine glasses per place setting—or have an additional supply stationed nearby, not back in the storage closet. Your guests will often switch back and forth between the red and the white wine; and two glasses are a must if you are going to offer two wines.

5. Instruct waiters that they are not to fill glasses more than half full unless specifically requested by the guest to pour a full glass. This will greatly reduce wastage and misspending.

6. Also instruct waiters that they must at all times inquire whether more wine is desired before pouring indiscriminately. Beware of free-pouring, cost-increasing service.

7. Wines are selected by the meeting planner and strict orders should be issued that if anyone desires to select his own wine, this is permissable only at personal expense. An individual check will have to be issued on the spot.

8. Wine service personnel should be instructed to carry a bottle of red in one hand and a bottle of white in the other, thus rendering prompt, polite, courteous service. I have nicknamed this type of service *airplane style* because the basic idea comes from the airlines.

THE PERFECT GIFT

Wine As A Gift

Wine sure beats hotel room service prices for hard liquor. For your guest speaker, key production qualifiers, top executives, or others who might merit VIP treatment, I recommend a nice bottle of red wine. If a spouse is involved—two wine glasses tied with a ribbon and a personal note of welcome or best wishes for a successful meeting is a nice touch.

Wine is always well received, particularly if you are not aware of the personal drinking habits of each VIP. It is a sure winner under such circumstances.

Wine As A Reward

Prompt return of a delegate's registration form (meeting questionnaire in my case) is vital to the success of my meeting planning
operation. Information pertaining to arrival and stayover plans,
name badge data, pre-registration information et al is on this form. In
the past several years I have tried to stimulate early returns of this
information by giving a bottle of wine with a personal note of thanks
to delegates who are prompt. The cost is modest, but the return on
this investment is great—delegates respond positively by getting their
meeting plans back to me on time.

SELECTION AND PRICING

Pricing

Standard hotel wine prices reflect a different type of service and
sales volume than that which takes place at a meeting, especially a
large one. Here there are no fancy buckets at each table, no need for
the hotel to train personnel in how to use a corkscrew, no tasting
ritual. Service personnel need not be highly trained or paid wine
stewards. This fact should put the meeting planner in a good position
to negotiate wine prices.

Hotels should realize that such wine service and the large
volume of wine so purchased does not warrant dining room wine list
prices. There should be a banquet wine list to enable a planner to buy
large quantities of wine at a fair and reasonable price. Unfortunately,
I have never encountered such a list and have always had to negotiate
a fair and reasonable price separately.

As the meeting planner becomes better acquainted with wine
and more sophisticated, a golden lesson is learned:

The best wine is not always the more expensive one.

The planner must seek an attractive price/value ratio. This comes with experience and good record keeping as to which wines your delegates like most.

House Wines

When making your wine selections be sure to check on the availability and quality of house wines (those that carry a hotel or house label). Frequently, the volume buying of the hotel will result in a quality wine under a house label at a very fine price to the customer. Most food and beverage directors will be more than happy to comment on the house wine they are serving.

Domestic vs. Foreign Wines

When meeting at home, American wines are a good buy. We have some great vineyards here in our own country.

The production of a grape variety varies greatly with soil and climate. The consistency of sunshine, temperatures, humidity, rainfall and rich soil in California makes many wines from this state an outstanding purchase from both a taste and price viewpoint. Because of overplanting in recent years, the grape crop is almost too big to squeeze; and some experts predict that in the next few years, due to oversupply, top quality California wine will be offered at some bargain prices. Keep this in mind when selecting your wines in the future.

Wines from the Erie Islands area, near Sandusky, Ohio, and upper New York State are the best known Eastern district wine areas.

If you are conducting a meeting in a foreign country, be sure to look into the domestic wines of that country. In any country, imported wines are subject to tax and duty charges to which domestic wines are not subject.

XVI

DINING ARRANGEMENTS

Eating is essential to the maintenance of life. If there were no other reason than to provide a human necessity a meeting planner would have to make arrangements for meals for meeting guests.

Meals in our culture, however, are more than a means of getting food to the point where the digestive tract can begin dispensing calories. Meals, especially dinners, are a social art form imbued with a special etiquette and traditional elegance.

You can show your guests how much you care—and give them something to remember—simply by serving them meals of excellent quality, perfectly prepared and beautifully presented. If you can do it all in an atmosphere of warm friendliness and social comraderie, you will have accomplished a major meeting planning objective. This is not easy to do.

NEED A BUFFET BE A BUFFET?

In today's environment of rising costs for food and labor, tight meeting schedules and the general inability of hotels to serve a group of people—particularly a group of 100 or more—"off the menu" with any degree of decorum and dignity, it is necessary for the professional meeting planner to challenge the traditional hotel methods of serving a meal.

Think of the usual hotel buffet: long lines . . . heavily loaded trays . . . overloaded dishes . . . anxious, tired people. It is not a very pretty picture—and it lacks class. If you want to give your guests a *treat* rather than a *treatment* of long lines and fatigue, apply a little imagination and creativity to a hotel's food presentations. Why not, for instance, a "sit down buffet" with wine service? The dining room personnel may not readily accept this format, but they will have to admit when you've explained it, that all you've done is combined aspects of a set menu with a basic buffet service approach. The mechanics of such meal service are really quite simple. Here is how it works:

Seating

Your cocktail party ends. Instead of heading for the buffet line, your guests seat themselves at round tables for six, eight or ten.

Table Settings

The tables are pre-set with ash trays, salt and pepper, flatware, poured ice water, a set appetizer (a nice fruit bowl or fish item, depending on the location and season) and a soup bowl. A hot consommé or soup will be served to all. Also, have a nice green salad at each setting with a choice of dressing on the table. Coffee cups should be placed at each setting.

Wine Service

I go one step further and include two wine glasses at each setting and I offer two moderately priced wines—a red and a white. Insist on two glasses as people tend to switch back and forth between the red and the white in the course of the evening.

Instruct the hotel staff to start pouring the wine as soon as the guests sit down. This eliminates the cocktail party withdrawal symptoms with which we are all familiar.

The wine should be served in the manner I call "airplane style." A server—who does not have to be a trained wine person—walks around with a bottle of red in one hand and a bottle of white in another. He simply asks your guests which they prefer.

If your budget doesn't permit the wine service, it can be eliminated, but try to keep it in because it really adds a lot! The cost is nominal based on your selection of wines and the price you have negotiated in advance.

Atmosphere

Be sure to give some thought to decorating your tables with candelabra and flowers or greens. Make your dinner set-up look elegant and it will be elegant! Soft background music also helps.

Buffet Entrees

Having started with as much of your table as possible pre-set, your dinner entrees (four to six choices) and vegetables can be served in standard buffet style. You will find that your guests regulate themselves in a smooth flow through the buffet line with no prodding or instruction from you—and, more importantly, from a sitting position rather than a long line.

Dessert

Why not incorporate a rolling dessert cart—or, at least, tray service with a choice of two or three items? This, again, allows guests to choose from a sitting position. Though it's a little more work for the staff, it's a great convenience for your guests! And they really appreciate it.

BUFFET BREAKFASTS

I borrowed this idea from Maurice A. (Moe) Belanger of Aetna Life and Casualty. The format is as follows:

Have a selection of fresh fruit, juices and danish pastries at the first station your guests encounter as they enter the dining room. And have coffee poured at the table as soon as they sit down with these items.

The personnel pouring the coffee should inform the guests that the main breakfast items (bacon, sausage, eggs, french toast, etc.) are located toward the rear or the center of the room. And *make sure the staff keeps pouring the coffee*—it's often the most important part of the breakfast.

The traditional buffet breakfast usually presents all items in one location. This alternative, however, provides a convenient, simple method for people to self-regulate themselves through the buffet line. After the first morning, lines disappear for the remainder of the meeting. You will also find that the main buffet items are used less and less as the meeting progresses. This results in tremendous breakage in the hotel's favor, providing a very good negotiating point as far as price and/or number of service personnel are concerned.

DINNER SEATING

It is common for meeting delegates to experience the "first day jitters." After all, they are in a strange physical environment, surrounded by what seems like a sea of strangers. These social pressures create anxiety which is expressed in many ways.

One such symptom is clearly evident during the first evening's reception. When there is no seating plan for dinner, delegates spend the entire reception hour worrying about where they will sit for dinner, and an abnormal amount of time is spent lining up dining partners. Confusion and nervousness reign; turned up chairs are everywhere. This situation is particularly probable at meetings where spouses are involved.

Planned dinner seating is the solution; it takes the burden off the delegates and places them in an atmosphere which is more conducive to getting to know and enjoying new people. Planned dinner seating can take many forms, but there are several that have worked well for me. Of the following, I would say that *seating by invitation* is most effectively used on the first evening while *seating by chance* works best on the second or third.

Dinner Seating By Invitation Or List

If you know in advance who is coming, assign each guest to a specific table. If you wish, assign a host as well. In this way you can issue invitations on the host's behalf to attending delegates. Another way, and one which simplifies the invitation process, is to place a list of table assignments in each delegate's portfolio.

Administrative instructions to the hotel when you are eating by plan are simple. Ask the maitre d' to set the dining room with tables of six, eight or ten place settings. Round tables are best as they are more intimate and conducive to good table discussion.

Next, number the tables one, two, three, four, etc. until the place settings equal the size of your group. Then issue dinner invitations according to table number, issuing as many invitations per table as you have place settings. This type of seating plan takes some time and work but your delegates will truly appreciate your efforts, especially on the first evening of a meeting.

Seating By Chance Draw

Seating by chance can be a lot of fun. Again your administrative instructions to the hotel are simple; just use the same table arrangements as those outlined above. All you have to do is place slips of paper with table assignments in a bowl and let people draw blindly for their dinner seats.

If the meeting does not include spouses, use one bowl. For tables set with eight place settings each, drop eight number ones, eight number twos, eight number threes, etc. into the bowl.

If the meeting does include spouses, let couples draw together and reduce the number of slips of paper accordingly so that one slip represents two settings. You will need a singles' bowl in addition to the couples' bowl because there will always be delegates who are either single or attending without their spouse.

Ideally, you will have delegates draw their table assignments during the reception period before dinner so that they can proceed immediately to their table when the reception ends. But if you do not have a reception, delegates can draw their table assignments as they enter the dining room.

I have used this kind of seating plan at meetings involving as few as 40 people or as many as 1,000. Most delegates enjoy the approach because it gives them a good chance to meet new people and eliminates anxiety. The planning, moreover, is simple; but be sure to give them the ground rules in advance.

By now you are saying, "Sure! Planned seating is great, but you can't do it every night of a meeting! People will feel too structured." I agree. At least one evening of a meeting people should be able to personally choose their dinner partners. But why not make it easy for them to do so . . .

Seating By Sign-Up

Seating by personal choice doesn't have to be free flow. Put up a "sign-up sheet" indicating the number of places available at each table with the appropriate number of spaces for people to sign their names. Do this early in the day and alert guests to review the board before they enter the dining room. Those delegates who have not specifically signed for a table should understand that it is up to them to fill in wherever there is an open place.

While this seating plan does not accomplish the objectives of removing social anxiety and making sure that everyone meets more of their fellow delegates, it is a lot better than just announcing that dinner will be free-flow and that they must make up their own table. Free-flow seating arrangements often result in complete chaos, unofficial "reserved" signs and, in some instances, hard feelings. Just to be safe, try sign-up seating towards the tail end of a meeting. By then people will know one another and will feel a lot more relaxed.

Free-Flow Seating

There is a place for free-flow dinner seating at a meeting. When you are having an open-ended, informal dress affair such as a western cook-out, a luau, a Bahamian Junkanoo or some other kind of theme party, an unstructured seating arrangement is the only system that makes sense.

XVII

MUSIC

Music was defined by St. Augustine in the fourth century as *the art of controlling or organizing sounds.* Most people will agree that this definition still holds true in our modern age. But music is also an important source of atmosphere and inspiration for a meeting; and the meeting planner must learn to control and organize music in such a way that it blends into and supports the essential purpose and objective of a meeting.

Take the traditional dinner dance frequently held at meetings which include spouses. Arrangements at first appear simple: hire an orchestra and make provisions for a dance floor. But the planner must do much more to keep his or her musical arrangements from making sour notes.

BASIC MUSICAL PLANNING

The planner must first evaluate the composition of the above dinner dancing audience in terms of age, musical tastes and style of dance they prefer. Will they respond favorably to the hustle, the fox-trot or disco? What kind of mixture will work best?

Secondly, the planner must realize that conversation is a part of any dinner dance. Music should not be so overwhelming that people cannot enjoy conversation at normal voice levels..

You must communicate your needs to the band leader or music agent to make absolutely sure that the band hired has the capability of playing a range of music that fits the variety of people in your audience. Ideally, you should observe the band playing for a similar group, though this is a luxury for which most planners will not find the time.

As a practical alternative, however, a planner can easily seek guidance from the hotel's management as to which bands have performed successfully at their hotel with similar groups. The planner can also speak to a professional production company, a band leader or a musical agent.

Musical arrangements must never be taken for granted!

Listen to professional advice; and if it is necessary to supplement the basic band with additional instruments to get the variety of music desired—do it! If you want a combination of the Lester Lanin sound and rock, recognize the need to add an electric guitarist and vocalist. It will cost more money, but is more than worth it—in terms of enjoyment.

You must also ascertain whether the band you have hired has ever worked the hotel before. Is the band leader willing and able to work with the food service personnel so as not to disrupt or impede food and beverage service? Does the band know *when* to play and *when not* to play? Does it know *what* to play? These questions must be asked—and answered.

And most importantly from the meeting planning point of view . . .

Musical needs must be clearly communicated and arrangements must be double checked to be sure they are understood and carried out.

GUIDELINES FOR USING MUSIC

The band must be playing as the group enters for dinner.

Usually a reception is held prior to a dinner dance. All the testing of microphones, amplifiers and instruments should have been checked out well in advance of dinner time. Sweet sounds of music should greet your guests as they arrive for dinner . . . not "testing, one, two, three."

While the meal is being served, if you have any doubt about the ability of the band leader to coordinate dance music with dinner service, instruct him not to play.

All that is required at this time is a little background music, so this is a good time for the band to take a break and leave only the piano player to gently tickle the ivories. Light piano music provides atmosphere, but permits meaningful dinner conversation.

Double check physical set-ups.

Acoustics are all-important. Be sure microphones work and that the sound system is properly adjusted. Amplifiers should be placed so that they are not blasting some tables right out of the room.

Insist on short dance sets.

Many couples are dancing just to be sociable or polite. Don't lock them in with long dance sets! A slight pause after a number is played is all that is required; but be sure to notify bandleaders of your needs in advance.

OTHER WAYS TO USE MUSIC

Recognition Programs

Live music can brighten any meeting. I often hire a trio to back up recognition programs. As each individual is called forth, appropriate music is played. For instance, if the delegate is from San Francisco . . . you guessed it, "I left my heart in San Francisco . . ."

Receptions

Strolling trios can also be very effective at receptions and cocktail parties. And for a final evening or a welcome evening do it up big with a high school band or some local musical extravaganza like the Jamaica Police Youth Band.

Part Five

DURING THE MEETING: ESSENTIALS AND EXTRAS

XVIII

MEDICAL
EMERGENCIES

Webster defines *emergency* as "an unforeseen combination of circumstances that call for immediate action." When the emergency is *medical,* the need for action is twice as pressing.

Medical emergencies are apt to occur at any time, usually the most inconvenient for the meeting planner. I have had experiences that range from flu to a contaminated water supply . . . from a serious cut on a foot in Jamaica to overexposure to the sun in Phoenix. Don't assume that it won't happen to you. It will! And both hotel staff and meeting planner must be prepared to handle medical emergencies quickly and efficiently.

Rare, however, is the hotel man who will say to you: "In the event of a medical emergency during your meeting, you should do the following . . ." Consider *yourself* responsible for medical arrangements for your meeting—and never assume that there is a procedure set up without asking in advance.

Written Instructions

Don't rely on hotel instructions which state: "We have a doctor on call. In case of emergency, call the switchboard and the operator will know the procedure." If you ask, the hotel can give *you* written instructions on how to get medical or dental assistance for attendees at your meeting.

There are many times when the regular house doctor is not available . . . or the telephone operator on duty at the moment may not know how to implement the hotel's so-called medical emergency procedure. This is especially apt to be true in the wee hours of the morning when so many emergencies occur!

Before your meeting, review the hotel's emergency procedure with the chief telephone operator—in the presence of a member of the hotel's management staff. And at the same time, obtain for your records: the name and phone number of the house doctor; the hours when he is available; and the name and phone number of his back-up.

Better still, meet the doctor himself before your meeting and go over the procedure. This is particularly helpful if you are meeting in a foreign country when the language barrier can prove extremely frustrating in an emergency situation.

MEDICAL EMERGENCY PLANNING CHECKLIST

In the event the hotel's basic procedure does not cover all possible situations, the meeting planner should develop a *Medical Emergency Planning Check List.* It should include the following information:

Procedure For Getting A Doctor
If the hotel's established procedure doesn't work, you need to have the names, addresses and phone numbers of the nearest doctors.

Procedure For Getting A Dentist
Names, addresses and phone numbers of nearby dentists.

Ambulance Service
Phone number; and distance and time it takes to get to the hotel.

Nearest Hospital

Name, address and phone number. It would also be helpful to have a map showing the easiest and shortest route to the hospital.

Drugstore

Is there a drugstore open at all hours? Name, address and phone number.

Emergency First-Aid

What facilities and/or persons knowledgeable in emergency techniques are available on the hotel premises or in close proximity?

Nursing Services

Is nursing service available at the hotel? Is there an infirmary to handle cuts and bruises that really don't require a doctor's care?

Transportation Source

If you do not have a car at your disposal 24 hours a day, make sure you know where to get one at a moment's notice.

With the hotel's cooperation and this *Medical Emergency Check List,* a planner should have a fail-safe program for medical emergencies or for any medical contingency at a meeting. Here's hoping you never have to implement such a plan; but it's going to happen some time, somewhere . . . so BE PREPARED.

XIX

PHOTOGRAPHY

The camera captures life's subtle and significant moments and furnishes us with cherished souvenirs of these events. Photographic coverage, therefore, is a powerful meeting tool—in terms of the dividends to be reaped by using it to recall the essence of a memorable meeting and as a simple but impressive means of recognizing and honoring the meeting's celebrities.

HOW TO USE PHOTOGRAPHY

Here are just some of the ways photography can be used to effectively point up a well-managed, unforgettable meeting:

Photo Place Cards

Using a self-processing camera, take informal shots of delegates as they are registering for the meeting. The photos can then be inserted in a card holder frame on which have been printed the name, date and location of the meeting along with a welcoming message.

While the delegates are attending the first evening's reception, place the souvenir photos on dinner tables to indicate assigned seats. They are a great icebreaker for the first dinner and help to get the meeting off to a fast start.

Another variation on this same theme is to take candid photos during the meeting and distribute them via the same placecard technique as a going home souvenir at the last evening's dinner.

Candid Shots

Photos of attendees at work and play presented following the meeting are wonderful mementos. Often such gifts are prominently displayed in homes and offices where they evoke pleasant memories.

"Memories Of Past Meetings" Slide Presentations

A photographic library of the highlights of past meetings can be built up using 35 mm slides. Then, on check-in day or at some other significant point during the meeting, run a "memories of past meetings" show. Such a presentation is simple, relatively inexpensive to run and extremely effective—"dynamite" impact at "firecracker" cost. And the slides can be easily converted to black and white or color photographs or serve themselves as special mementos.

Portraits

Many firms do charcoal drawings or colored portrait reproductions of photographs. Properly framed with an appropriate inscription, these serve as a substantive remembrance or recognition item.

Group Photographs

Once a tradition, the group photograph is making a comeback. The largest of groups can be taken with a panorama camera; but for smaller groups, simpler cameras are just as effective and less expensive.

Transparency Vu-Graphs—Lucite Frames

An 8 x 10 transparency can be made from any color slide or negative and flashed on a screen using an overhead projector. After the program the transparency can be slipped into a lucite frame to which an engraved plate recognizing the recipient's achievement has been attached.

"Meet Your Leaders" Gallery

Important attendees—sales leaders, top management, award winners—can be saluted and introduced by mounting their photographs on a prominent gallery board. The cost is minimal but it is a great build-up for the leaders and a "who's who" information center for the other delegates.

Autographed Recognition Photographs

On numerous occasions, meeting delegates are recognized for significant achievements—like a special anniversary or an outstanding sales record. Portraits of these persons can be blown up, mounted on hardboard and displayed on easels. As they enter the meeting, other delegates can be asked to sign the photos. The portrait with the various signatures can then be attractively framed and mounted with a commemorative plate; and, for a modest price, the honored delegate has a very special personal gift.

Veiled Award Portraits

The blown-up photo technique can also be used to announce award winners with veiled photographs of the winners placed on separate easels. As winners are announced from the podium and come forward to receive their awards, photographs of the presentation are taken and the individual's portrait is unveiled. The veils are a real attention getter and audience tension builds as each portrait is uncovered. Again, following the ceremony, the blow-ups can be framed and presented to the winners.

Documentation Of Attendance

Photographs of meetings involving delegates and spouses go a long way to visually document the importance and necessity of spouse attendance at meetings. Photographs of major business sessions are also tangible proof of the serious nature of these programs.

There are two golden rules for good photographic coverage:

Hire A Pro

Get written agreement on prices and services to be performed. Give clear instructions along with adequate supervision and direction —and let the professional photographer do the job!

Keep It Simple

When dealing with colored slides, especially presentations on the site, use simply processed film such as Ektachrome. Highly sophisticated film merely involves greater complication and added expense.

THREE SOURCES
TO GET THE JOB DONE

It is the meeting planner's job to contract for the services that make meetings successful. The three main sources of professional photographic coverage are: a professional member of your own meeting planning staff; an on-site photographer; or a free lance professional.

Professional Staff Member

Without question, the ideal way to handle photographic coverage and related support services is to have a professional on your own planning staff. If the meeting planning operation is centralized and handles a sufficient number of meetings, such a staff person is economically prudent, for in addition to on-the-spot coverage, he or she can handle basic meeting room set-up, sound adjustment, taping, audiovisual staffing, meeting registration and similar on-site duties.

Because of the size of their operation or the relatively small number of meetings they conduct, however, many planners do not have such a staff person available and other alternatives must be found. Unfortunately, hiring a photographer is a further complication of the planner's function, for the photographer must be thoroughly briefed and supervised.

Hotel/Local Meeting Site Photographer

One alternative is to engage the services of a local photographer with whom the hotel regularly does business. During the initial inspection and planning visit to the site, consult with the hotel's management as to their opinion of the local photographer in light of your particular needs. Does he have the expertise to do the job? And can good performance be bought at a reasonable price?

There are obviously some advantages to dealing with a hotel/local photographer. You eliminate the expenses for travel, room and board, etc. you would have had if you had used your own staff professional. You also normally have the advantage of handy processing facilities.

But the disadvantages are that a local/hotel photographer will not know which of your people are important and your planning job becomes more complicated as you add the supervision of a photographer and other audiovisual personnel to your other functions. Very often, only photographic services can be bought from the photographer—and you must look elsewhere for persons to handle other communications tasks.

Free Lance Professional

If you have worked successfully with a particular photographer at one hotel site, you may be able to hire him for other sites in that general geographical area. Often the romance of travel and the opportunity to see other hotel facilities will make the person willing to work for a reasonable fee.

PHOTOGRAPHIC
HIRING AND PRICING

Meet personally with a photographer who has been recommended and explain your needs and expectations. Check the photographer's ability to put on a slide show and summary of your meeting and the availability of slide projectors, dissolve units and labor costs to run such equipment. Ask for the names of meeting planners the photographer has worked with in the past and be sure to check these references for opinions of work performed in light of expenditures.

From a free lance or local photographer get prices on both an hourly basis and a per roll basis; black and white versus color; processing costs for color slides, etc. Check into the possibility of buying contact sheets and negatives if you want a selection of films to process at home and send out as souvenirs.

Keep in mind that posted price quotes from the typical hotel photographer for items such as key chain viewers, 3½ x 5 prints or 5 x 7 enlargements are prices based on *speculation*. The photographer expects only a percentage of his photos to be bought and his posted prices reflect this speculation. If you *guarantee* the purchase of a certain number that price should and will be substantially reduced.

As a meeting planner, photography and audiovisual support should be a major part of your planning. In spite of the fact that it can be time consuming and complicated, photography is an extremely important meeting tool and is well worth the effort. Remember—a picture is worth a thousand words!

Part Six

AFTER THE MEETING:
REVIEW AND REWARD

XX

ACCOUNTING

One of the major complaints made by meeting planners concerns hotel accounting procedures and documentation. Planners refer to it as "that accounting mess," for hotel accounting, it seems, never gets done the way the planner wants or his or her organization requires.

A majority of the accounting problems, however, actually begin with the meeting planner. Too often, he or she fails to recognize the fact that

A major part of the meeting planning function is to assume specific accounting responsibilities during the meeting itself.

The planner must recognize that this is a job that must be performed in an efficient, orderly manner—and on time!

Good accounting procedures must be set up—and a review schedule established—during the negoti- ating and planning stages of the meeting.

Ground rules for accounting must be negotiated and spelled out early in the game. Prior to confirmation, there must be a clear agreement as to which charges will be posted to the master account during the meeting—when—and in what format.

MEETING ACCOUNTING RESPONSIBILITIES

During the meeting, the planner's accounting responsibilities fall into two basic areas:

(1) Review of the organization's master account
(2) Review of the charges posted to the individual portfolios of meeting delegates.

Both of these responsibilities can be fulfilled at the same time!

Daily Review Of Master Account

A daily review of the prior day's master account charges is an essential meeting accounting procedure. The planner should specifically request that all charges for a given day be posted to the master account for review the following day. This system forces the various departments of the hotel to submit charges to the master account *on time* and *regularly*.

It is best that charges be posted daily and in sequence with your basic schedule of events. Master account charges should also be expressed in terms that you, the meeting planner, understand. Instead of merely listing the number of drinks and hors d'oeuvres consumed on a certain day, for instance, it would be far better to have the master account read as follows:

OPENING NIGHT RECEPTION COSTS—1979 MANAGEMENT CONFERENCE
  Liquor—X dollars, plus tax and gratuity
  Hors d'oeuvres—X dollars, plus tax and gratuity

Each master account entry must be backed up with suitable documentation which explains the charge.

If you follow this day-by-day review schedule, you can be assured of approving master account charges when everyone's memory is fresh. And any misunderstanding or disagreements can be worked out before any accounting problems accumulate.

Arrange a schedule for this review that fits your own personal habits. I, for example, happen to be an early riser and find that my most productive time of day is the early morning. So I review daily master account charges every morning at 7:15 in my room where all of my records are readily available. I feel that at this hour I have the benefit of a good night's sleep and feel refreshed.

Daily Review Of Individual Portfolios
The second major accounting responsibility—making sure that delegates are being charged the agreed-upon hotel rate and applicable taxes and gratuities—can be accomplished at the same time you review the master account simply by making a daily random sampling of individual accounts.

On check-in day, provide the accounting manager with a list of ten or fifteen individual accounts to be reviewed the next day. The list should span the alphabet from A to Z. It takes only a few minutes to ascertain whether agreed-upon charges are being properly posted. And in the event charges are not being properly posted, corrections can be made well in advance of check-out time—thus eliminating a potential meeting negative.

Provide the accounting manager with a new list of accounts to be reviewed each day. To save time during the meeting, these lists can be prepared in advance; but distribute them to the accounting manager on a day by day basis, not all at once.

Be sure the list of accounts to be reviewed includes all of the different accounting situations with which the front office might be confronted. These would include:

Mr. & Mrs. Account (husband and wife on one portfolio)
This portfolio should indicate the double occupancy rate plus applicable tax and gratuities.

Single Account
This portfolio should reflect the single occupancy rate plus applicable tax and gratuities.

Mr. & Mr. or Ms. & Ms. Account (two people sharing one room)
This portfolio should show two persons sharing the agreed-upon double occupancy rate. Each will be assigned one-half of the double occupancy plus applicable tax and gratuities.

Children Sharing A Room With Parents
This is an obvious portfolio to check if there are agreed upon special rates being charged for children in this situation.

Suite Accommodations
If suites are being utilized, these portfolios should be checked to see if they show the proper rates, taxes and gratuities.

Random samplings of these cost portfolios pay handsome dividends in terms of a smooth check-out for attendees at the conclusion of the meeting. Nothing is worse than having a meeting's success destroyed at the last minute because billing instructions have not been followed by the front desk in their preparation of the cost portfolios. Firsthand review of what the clerks at the front desk are actually doing is necessary. It is not enough to read the hotel specification sheets. By establishing an orderly daily procedure this major responsibility can be discharged painlessly.

XXI

GRATUITIES

The word *tips,* an acronym for "To Insure Prompt Service," was coined in 1487 by the Marquis de Sailby upon noting that a token above the agreed price would insure speedy service in his London tailor shop. The Marquis, unfortunately or otherwise, thus established a custom which was henceforth to plague the service industries which adopted it.

Although the concept was clear—to stimulate service—several major questions were left unanswered:

Which employees should be tipped?
How much should they be tipped?
When and how should they be tipped?

We are still wrestling with these complicated questions today. One of the most difficult and delicate tasks a meeting planner performs is ensuring that his or her organization's gratuity dollars are properly disbursed and receive the proper return in terms of service quality and employee attitude. Distribution of gratuities, in fact, is one of the most important aspects of a meeting's financial planning.

TIPPING GUIDELINES

It is difficult to draw firm guidelines that will fit each gratuity situation for practices vary from site to site and from organization to organization. There are, however, certain steps a meeting planner *must* take before confirming any meeting.

The planner must make clear to hotel management that all gratuities are based on the premise of good and prompt service.

The planner must secure agreement that gratuities are not automatic and that hotel management will guarantee that the service for which the planner is paying is rendered.

Even operating on a blanket basis, the meeting planner should make it clear that his or her organization will not pay these gratuities if the agreed-upon service is not forthcoming. If the management of a hotel doesn't have enough faith in its staff to make such a commitment, then the planner should look elsewhere.

Blanket Gratuities: Pro and Con

Blanket gratuities, covering the tipping for an entire meeting, are common; the concept is basically a sound one—its purpose being to assure all meeting attendees of uniform good service. Ideally, the blanket tip should eliminate such problems as the non-tipper or the big-tipper; and it should alleviate any anxiety on the part of a meeting delegate about who, what or when to tip. A blanket arrangement should stimulate the hotel staff to do a superior job because of prompt and generous payment for the services they render. But . . .

To assure a proper return on gratuity expenditures, the meeting planner must carefully ascertain where every blanket gratuity dollar is going—and what his or her organization is getting for the money.

The planner must evaluate the hotel's proposed gratuity arrangement as carefully as he does its room and food charges. And if a hotel man attempts the "of course, we apply a 15% gratuity charge to cover all services" approach, a red flag should immediately go up.

Sad to say, sales managers and general managers in some of the finest hotels often have to fumble for an explanation of where all the money does go. For the fact of the matter is that in the majority of instances it does not go to the staff who actually serviced the group. *Very often, the blanket procedure is either a wage subsidization program or higher rate in disguise.*

In actual practice, for instance, some hotels distribute no gratuities to dining room personnel. They give as an explanation for charging you dining gratuities but not distributing them the fact that they pay their hotel employees a higher hourly wage than they otherwise would . . . and use these gratuities to offset their additional labor costs. This is not a desirable program in which to participate!

I have found that blanket "gratuities" have been used by hotels to offset bad debts; that "gratuities" have been thrown into the general management fund; or that the difference between gratuities actually paid and gratuities charged goes directly into the hotel coffers as standard revenue.

Individual vs. Group Tipping

Before you can engage in any meaningful discussion of group or blanket gratuity arrangements, you must ascertain how an individual guest tips—and whether the hotel provides individual guests with practical tipping guidelines.

As a general rule, you want to tip, as a *minimum,* as much as the average individual guest—and in the majority of cases, *more.* Hotel management and staff then know that you are not a "bunch of stiffs," but a generous organization willing to pay for superior service.

You must insist, however, that hotel management get this message across to their people. And you must check *before* and *during* your meeting that this has, in fact, been accomplished.

As a general rule, a meeting planner should NOT pay a flat 15% on a Full American Plan, Modified American Plan or European Plan rate.

Let us say you are given a Full American Plan rate of $90 a day, double occupancy, or $45 a day per person. Your first job is to ascertain how much of this $45 each day is allocated toward meal expenses—breakfast, lunch and dinner. A typical pattern might be: breakfast—$4; lunch—$5; dinner—$11. A total food allocation, in this instance, of $20.

My experience has been that dining room staff—waitresses, captains and maitre d's—are actually distributed gratuities on the basis of 15% of $20, or $3 per day per person. Breaking this down on a per meal basis, it would be: breakfast—60¢; lunch—75¢; dinner— $1.65 (total—$3).

If you are taking a large group to the hotel, let us say 500 people, you are talking about a large amount of money for gratuities on this basis. The question you must ask yourself is: "Are individual guests paying more or less than this amount?" You will likely find that they are tipping *less*.

To stimulate good service, if we were to say that individual guests tip approximately that amount per day, you *might* be better off to grant an extra 25¢ per person per day to dining room staff.

On the other hand, taking the above example further, $25 of the $45 per day FAP is a room charge. If you were to allow the hotel to apply a blanket 15% to the entire FAP rate, you would be paying an additional $3.75 per day per person. The question now is: "If you do this, where does the money go? And is it a worthwhile investment?"

My experience has been that if this amount is distributed, it actually goes to personnel who should not necessarily be tipped, or perhaps to personnel who do not merit gratuity consideration. Therefore . . .

The meeting planner should specifically direct as many gratuity dollars as possible.

GRATUITY DISTRIBUTION
AND COMMUNICATION

You can be flexible in terms of the basic arrangements you make from hotel to hotel. But you must be completely rigid with regard to the importance of good communication of tipping arrangements to your company's guests and the hotel staff members who will serve them.

Make absolutely sure that whatever arrangements are made, they are clearly spelled out to your meeting attendee.

The meeting planner has sole responsibility to the hotel's management and to the meeting attendees to make sure that everyone knows the rules of the game. If this is accomplished, an important step has been taken in setting up the framework for a successful meeting. What follows are some examples of the way I typically outline gratuity arrangements for my attendees.

Housekeeping

Maid and housekeeping services are very often the lowest paid of the hotel's staff. They are, as well, frequently overlooked or improperly tipped. Since no one renders the guest more direct, timely and necessary service, I will often be more generous than the hotel recommends in this area. My own *minimum* guideline is 50¢ per person per day, or $1 per room occupied, and an additional $1 per day minimum for suite facilities.

I use the term "maid and housekeeping" when turning these gratuities over to the hotel because it automatically gives the management the flexibility to distribute some of the funds to inspectresses, supervisory personnel and housemen who assist the maid in her duties. You should, however, double check the hotel management's method of communicating to the housekeeping staff that they are receiving your gratuities.

In some hotels, such as a large commercial hotel with 1,000 or more rooms, you might be occupying only 200. A good way to make sure you are getting your money's worth and that the word is getting through to the housekeeping staff is to place the following card—having cleared it with management first, of course—in each of the rooms assigned to your guests.

ATTENTION MAID

As a guest of your hotel, I certainly appreciate the fine service you render.

In gratitude for your efficient and timely service during my stay, my company, _____, will pay a generous service gratuity which includes maid and housekeeping gratuities . . . our thanks to you for a job well done!

These gratuities will be distributed by your hotel management. If you have any questions, please contact your supervisor who has been advised of this arrangement.

_____

(signature)

You might inform attendees at your meeting of coverage for housekeeping gratuities with the following:

Your maid, inspectress and assisting housemen are all covered by a blanket daily service charge of 75¢ per day per person. This arrangement applies to early arrivals and stayovers as well as for the official meeting period.

Please do not tip in addition to the amount provided by the basic service charge.

Meals

As far as meal gratuities are concerned, you should be equally specific that, on a per person basis, you are paying gratuities that cover the maitre d', the captain and all dining room personnel—and list the specific amounts broken down on a per meal basis. Again, admonish attendees *not* to tip in addition to the amounts you are providing.

Luggage Handling

I generally try *not* to include the hotel doormen and bellmen in my blanket gratuity arrangements; and for the majority of meetings, this is acceptable to the hotel. The reason I don't place luggage handling under the blanket gratuity is that I personally find it very difficult not to tip for this service, and I am sure that most of my delegates do also. Thus duplicate tipping occurs and, consequently, overpayment for services actually rendered.

When luggage handling in and out of the hotel is not covered and my people will be personally responsible for tipping the bellman or doorman, I notify them as follows:

> Gratuities for those handling your luggage in and out of the hotel are not covered by the blanket service charge. Each of you will be personally responsible for tipping for this service.
>
> HOTEL DOORMAN—Tip according to service rendered. The doorman who welcomes you to the hotel and assists you in unloading your luggage from the taxi should be tipped 50¢—$1, depending on the number of bags.
>
> HOTEL BELLMAN—Be sure to tip!—The bellman who will transport your luggage to and from your room should be tipped 50¢ per large suitcase and 25¢ per handbag. A minimum guideline of $1 in and $1 out per couple should be followed.

When working this type of arrangement where each delegate is personally responsible for luggage handling tips, I set up with hotel management, behind the scene, a minimum guarantee of $1 per couple in and out of the hotel. Then, all the bellman must do if someone forgets to tip is to notify the bell captain and give him the room number of the guest who did not tip.

In the event someone does not tip, I inquire as to why. Often there are some very good reasons—such as rude service—of which the bell captain should be apprised. And obviously, if it is such a reason, the $1 guaranteed minimum is not paid! If, however, the guest only inadvertently forgot to tip, I authorize the bell captain to reimburse the bellman. By setting up this kind of safeguard, you can end any complaints about the money received from any of your groups.

Due to union regulations or long-standing tradition in some hotels, however, you may occasionally find that a blanket amount for in-and-out service **is required.** When such a situation prevails, guests must be notified as follows:

> To each individual's bill, a service charge of $1.75—$3.50 per couple—will be added to cover luggage handling services in and out of the hotel. This amount covers the doorman, the bell captain and the bellman who takes your luggage to and from your room.
>
> This is a union requirement in the hotel and the amount is a generous one. You should expect and get good service. Identify yourself as being with our company. Should you encounter any instance of a "hands out" attitude or a pretense of not being aware of this blanket arrangement, report this immediately to the company's service desk.
>
> This blanket service charge for luggage handling applies to early arrivals and/or stayovers as well.
>
> Please do not tip in addition to the basic service charge.

GRATUITIES NOT COVERED

A number of services that require gratuities are most often not covered in a blanket gratuity arrangement. Attendees should always be informed of these services and provided with guidelines for their own use. Some examples follow:

Beverage Service

> If you order liquor or wine in the dining room, cocktail lounge, at poolside or elsewhere, you are personally responsible for the tip involved.
>
> Assuming, good service, we recommend 15%.

Personal Services

Should you require any special personal services such as those of room service, valet or barber shop, you should take care of the necessary tips. Here are some helpful guidelines:

Barber — 50¢-$1
Beauty Parlor — 15%-20% of charge
Coat Check — 25¢ each garment
Room Service — 15% of charge
Taxicab — 10%-15% of charge
Telegrams and messages — 50¢-$1
Valet — 50¢-75¢ on pick-up; $1 upon return
Skycaps and porters at airports — 25¢ per bag
Poolboy — 25¢ per set-up

SPECIAL GRATUITIES

Special gratuities are tips in excess of, or in addition to, amounts paid out under blanket gratuity arrangements. Very frequently, people who are key to the success of your meeting are not covered—or, at least, are not adequately covered—by a blanket arrangement.

For example, you might find that dining room captains and the maitre d' are excluded from the 15% meal gratuity. Or that key meeting supporters—such as the head houseman and his staff—are not included in the blanket arrangement. Yet these are the service people who could make or break your meeting. They should receive gratuities!

Special gratuities *must* be distributed to recognize truly superior service beyond the call of duty—even to people who *are* covered under the blanket arrangements. Special gratuities can be looked upon as a vehicle for showing appreciation of service you would not normally expect or for an unusual need that you may anticipate.

The gal in the hotel sales office who types long into the night on a speaker's presentation that should have been done prior to his arrival at the hotel . . . the house staff that must suddenly reset a meeting room due to last minute changes . . . these people deserve your recognition of a job well done. The difficulty is in deciding *who* is eligible for a special gratuity? *How much* and *how to distribute* are equally troublesome. The following guidelines may prove helpful.

Who

Early discussion

At the time of the initial booking and planning of a meeting you should discuss with hotel management the concept of special gratuities as they understand it in their hotel. What are their customs and/or general attitude on the subject? Based on your meeting program, who do they think might deserve special gratuity consideration? And based on the size of your meeting, what dollar range, . assuming top performance, do they recommend?

Review

Just before the meeting begins—and you should routinely arrive a minimum of one day (preferably two) in advance of the beginning of a major meeting—review your earlier discussion with the hotel's management team to be assured that you are still in tune and that circumstances have not changed.

Following the meeting, hold a *constructive review* session with hotel management as well as with other service organizations, such as ground transportation companies, who have been involved in the meeting.

Then independently, after consultation with members of your own staff, make a list of people who in your judgment merit special gratuity consideration and list the amount you feel is appropriate. Make a list as well of the hotel's recommendations of people and suggested amounts.

Open Discussion

Now, in open discussion, you share your list. It might run like this . . .

"Bill is extremely well paid and not traditionally tipped."

"Please don't tip Jack. I don't want to establish a precedent."

"Carol went out of her way and it's not her normal job. She should definitely be tipped."

On and on it goes, both parties giving input.

Take Time

Don't make any immediate decisions! Fatigue and letdown set in following a strenuous and successful meeting. You are tired—but you still have a lot to do. Don't make a final judgment at this time. Sleep on it and make decisions the next day.

Once these decisions are made, share your original thoughts with hotel management. And draw up another column on your list— "approved dollar amount."

How To Pay Special Gratuities

Walking around the hotel playing Santa Claus handing out money would make me feel uncomfortable and unprofessional. Instead I authorize a *master account payout,* placing distribution responsibilities on hotel management who must certify via signatures that the monies have been distributed as indicated. There are a number of reasons for this procedure: Often a lot of money is involved; and I must account for this expenditure to my company. The procedure fulfills my corporate accounting requirements.

Take the time to handwrite, on your own stationery or business card, a note of thanks to each employee who is to receive a special gratuity. These notes are distributed by hotel management along with the gratuities. You also want to give hotel management an opportunity to thank, in your organization's behalf, employees who have exerted themselves and done a good job. The distribution should take place after you have left the hotel, if only because you feel—as I do—that you don't want hotel employees stopping you in the hall and thanking you for something that they have really earned.

As a rough guideline, I budget $1 per person attending the meeting for special gratuities. Often, however, I am above or below this figure, depending on the hotel property I am working and the total circumstances of the meeting being conducted.

For Those Who Can't Be Tipped

Telephone Operators

What do you do about people who have done an outstanding job in assisting with a successful meeting, but who can't or shouldn't be tipped? It would be hard, for instance, to give a meaningful gratuity to the telephone operators because there are so many of them.

What I have used for a staff of this kind is the "flower and card" approach. The day before the meeting is to start, send flowers and candy to the telephone operating staff with a note that goes something like the following . . .

> The (name of company) **will be conducting their** (name of meeting) **meeting during** (meeting dates) **at your hotel, and I just want you folks to know that we realize how important your job is to the success of our meeting. Thanks for doing a good job!**

> _____
> (signed)

Needless to say, we usually get very efficient and courteous telephone service.

Hotel Management

The best way to thank hotel management is with repeat business and your active good will, like referring others to the hotel. This pays great dividends in terms of the type of service your groups receive. Letters are important, but be sure they are sincerely earned. Don't become a "good guy Charlie" letter writer who doesn't mean what he says.

Hotel managers often are married and have families, and you might consider writing a thank-you note to the wife or husband who's spouse has spent long evenings assisting you. You might also think about inviting members of hotel management and their spouses to a facility outside of their own hotel as your guest for a word of thanks in a relaxed environment.

When the general manager or the salesperson who worked so

hard on your meeting happens to be in your community, make absolutely sure that he or she is your guest for lunch or dinner. Your door and your telephone line should be open, regardless of how busy you are.

Tipping need not be a can of worms. It is, however, a delicate system that must be continuously checked and reviewed. Once you have established clear guidelines and communicated them to all concerned, you will have built a foundation for a successful meeting. Remember, your gratuity arrangements are your organization's basic recognition and motivation system for the people servicing you.

XXII

POST-MEETING EVALUATION

An important part of the meeting planner's work is the evaluation of the product—the meeting itself. A formal meeting review system must be established to develop a truly professional meeting planning operation.

I found, in checking with other meeting planners, that few had a formalized review system. Those that did have one used it only sporadically and did not devote a significant amount of time or money to post-meeting evaluation. I had followed a similar path, and experimented with a wide variety of post-meeting evaluation techniques, including written reports from home office executives attending the session, statistical samplings of delegates by written questionnaires, random samplings by phone and post-meeting critique and planning sessions with invited delegates. None of these seemed totally adequate.

EVALUATION QUESTIONNAIRE

In 1976, however, I implemented a meeting evaluation report

program at major corporate meetings and asked all delegates to participate. A copy of the *Meeting Evaluation Report Questionnaire* is included at the end of this chapter.

A close look at this questionnaire might help you to develop an evaluation report form that meets your specific needs. It meets my criteria in the following ways:

1.) The format is self-explanatory and simply laid out. It can be filled out quickly and easily without a lot of administrative instructions.
2.) The scoring key is specific and is indicated both numerically and verbally permitting delegates to express themselves accurately. By using a two-number index evaluation (i.e. 4-5-fairly good), shades of enthusiasm can be easily expressed.

This report form is designed for use at all types of meetings, whether delegates only or delegate/spouse. It can also be used by all meeting attendees. It should be noted, moreover, that the spouse's evaluation will often vary greatly from the delegate's. This is particularly true in areas of program format and content, meals and service.

Site Evaluation

Data from the conference site evaluation section is of great assistance to the meeting planner in his or her feedback to the hotel; and it strengthens the meeting planner's position with the hotel, whether the response is positive or negative.

An evaluation of the site is especially helpful if future meetings are scheduled at the same hotel. If planning meetings is a centralized function in the company, meeting sites already used will inevitably come up for consideration by other departments or subsidiaries. If a client is contemplating a meeting site that, based on prior experience did not live up to expectations, the planner can advise the client of the nonfavorable evaluations and even suggest a quick look through the files to confirm the position. On the other hand, if the experience at a particular site was good, the reports serve as a powerful third-party influence which objectively substantiates the personal opinion of the planner.

Business Program Evaluation

The evaluation of the business program reflects whether it was noticeably good or obviously bad. The response is usually heavily weighted in one direction or the other. The guest speaker, if one is involved, is a hit or a flop; and the planned social and recreational activities are either well received or not. In other words, the reponse to the program is seldom neutral.

Communications Evaluation

The section of the report on communications gives insight into the effective performance of the conference planning operation. The advance release and all meeting kit information, including programs, guest list, name badges, dinner invitations, etc., are generally prepared by the planner and his or her assistants. Evaluation scores in this area should be consistently high if the planner has full and complete control over this area.

Three Highlights

Requesting three highlights of the meeting gives the planner an idea of what is being done right, particularly if the same items are repeated on several forms. It is a good source of ideas that should be applied to future meetings.

Suggested Improvements

The section on areas for improvement will often hurt a little but comments tend to substantiate most major things you already know went wrong or which you realized were not too desirable to start with. They confirm the need to plan more carefully in certain areas.

Interestingly enough, the highlights and areas for improvements can provide the planner with documented answers for people who take an extreme position on a particular feature of a meeting. For example, I often use assigned seating by invitation for dinners. One delegate vehemently complained about this. However, I was able to show that a large number of delegates at previous meetings rated the seating assignments as a favorable point because this approach gave them an opportunity to meet new people and did away with the anxiety which sometimes accompanies making dinner plans during a meeting. The critic changed his mind, but without the evaluation reports to document the feelings of others, it is doubtful that he would have done so.

Suggestions And Comments

The section of the report for suggestions and comments can provide a meaningful, constructive line of communication between the planner and the delegates. More often, however, it is a cheer leading section with comments like "Keep up the good work," "More of the same," or "See you next year." Remember too that delegates might make suggestions that cannot be implemented because of legal or corporate policy.

The optional signature feature assures a more open communication. Some people express themselves more freely when they are not identified by their signature. Generally the report sets up a formal communication channel separate from the emotional environment of the meeting. It serves as a good release mechanism for the feelings and opinions of your meeting delegates.

Importance Of Evaluation

Planners might consider including in the advance release on the meeting an explanation of the importance of the evaluation report as a vehicle for planning and conducting better meetings. The importance of completing the form could also be emphasized from the podium the first and last day of the meeting.

Further evaluations of the meeting could be conducted in several ways. Each meeting could be reviewed with the planning staff for suggestions on how planning and administering the meeting's program could have been more efficient and effective. Each supplier of service, the hotel, guest speakers, etc., could be asked to give a written critique regarding the manner in which the staff worked with them. These sources might have suggestions on improving working relationships and program plans.

A statistical summary of the meeting evaluation reports should be given to the sponsoring department and/or subsidiary company. In addition, a meeting to review the evaluation results with the department head for whom the meeting was planned might be helpful to both parties. Specific plans and goals for the next meeting could be based on lessons learned from the reports. The results of the evaluation should be compiled in a report and made a part of the next meeting's file.

Post-meeting evaluation, to date, has not been a strong point for many planners. More attention, however, is now being given to this important area; and a sharing of information in this relatively new field could be beneficial to all planners.

MEETING EVALUATION REPORT FORM

Please complete the following *Evaluation Report.* Your constructive criticism will help to plan better meetings.

Scoring Key
7-6 Excellent
5-4 Good
3-2 Fair
1-0 Poor

Name of meeting _____

My spouse attended: Yes _____ No _____

	Delegate Response	Spouse Response
Conference Site		
Location	_____	_____
Lodging	_____	_____
Meals	_____	_____
Service	_____	_____

Service   _____   _____

Staff Attitude   _____   _____

Meeting Rooms   _____   _____

Recreational Facilities   _____   _____

Program

Content (Meaningful)   _____   _____

Format (Interesting, varied)   _____   _____

Guest Speaker   _____   _____

Social Activities

Social Activities   _____   _____

Recreation Activities   _____   _____

Communications

Advance Meeting Information Release   _____   _____

Meeting Kit Contents   _____   _____

General

State the three major meeting highlights from your viewpoint.

State the three areas where we could most improve the value of the
meeting.

Suggestions & Comments
(Use reverse side if necessary)

_____

_____

_____

_____

_____

_____

_____

_____

_____

_____

_____

_____

Signature Optional

CONCLUDING
THOUGHTS

Meeting planning is as much an art as a science. The successful meeting planner is a unique person. In time meeting planning will be formally recognized as a profession; and it is hoped that this book will assist in making that day come soon.

This book should serve not only as a reference for meeting planners in their day to day activities, but also as a vehicle to build prestige within their employing organizations. It should be shared with influential members of their organizations, for it should serve as an excellent "third party" in explaining the myriad details and complexities that must be coped with to conduct a successful meeting.

Education is the key to gaining professional recognition. The rapid growth of Meeting Planners International (MPI) in membership and financial resources affords this fine organization a tremendous opportunity—*to become the driving force that brings professionalism and proper recognition to the meeting planning field.* To do so, MPI must work just as hard at educating organizations as to the value and importance of their meeting planners as it does at educating the planner on how to do the job better.

Meeting planning techniques and procedures can be taught; and I urge the colleges and universities of America to continue striving to build curricula that will provide sound foundations for future meeting planners.

I also urge our business leaders—both corporate and association —to re-evaluate meeting activity and meeting planning staffs in order to be assured that they are being as effective as possible in this vital area of communication and service.

This book is just a beginning as far as providing the educational tools a professional meeting planner must have. More books must be written to update the ever changing world of the meeting planner. Perhaps the future authors have just finished reading this book. If so, I hope they will start now to put their thoughts and experiences in writing.

James E. Jones

APPENDIX

CHECK LIST
AND
MEETING PLAN

In 1972, a joint committee of planners and hotel executives—of which Silas Cline of the Penn Mutual Life Insurance Company and I were members—developed the following *Check List and Meeting Plan*. Its purpose is simple: to aid the meeting planner to prepare for and cope with the multitude of arrangements and situations which are part of any meeting or convention.

The *Check List* section covers information that should be obtained about a site during the inspection trip and is an excellent source of documentation of facilities. The statistics contained therein can be used for a comparison of properties as well as for making the final arrangements when the site has been selected. The *Meeting Plan* section—which deals with registration, meals, receptions, programs and special events—includes sheets to be filled out for the various daily functions and schedules.When all details have been appropriately documented the end result is a total meeting plan book.

I recommend that two copies of the *Check List* be sent to a hotel in advance of an inspection visit. One of them should be filled out and waiting for you at the registration desk upon arrival. It is impossible to overestimate the value of this list in terms of its contribution to a successful meeting.

CHECK LIST

General Hotel Information

DATE _____

NAME OF HOTEL _____

ADDRESS _____

CONTACT _____PHONE _____

NUMBER OF ROOMS	_____	TELEX	_____
NUMBER OF COTTAGES	_____	CAPACITY	_____
NEAREST TOWN	_____	DISTANCE	_____
NEAREST AIRPORT	_____	DISTANCE	_____
CHECK IN TIME	_____	CHECK OUT TIME	_____

HOTEL OPERATES ON □ EASTERN □ CENTRAL □ MOUNTAIN □ PACIFIC TIME

AIR CONDITIONED □ ROOMS □ PUBLIC SPACE □ MEETING ROOMS

PARKING □ INSIDE □ OUTSIDE □ SELF PARKING

☐ VALET PARKING _____ COST

AUTO RENTAL □ YES □ NO   NAME OF COMPANY _____

TRANSPORTATION	FROM AIRPORT	FROM TRAIN
COST OF TAXI	_____	_____
COST OF LIMOUSINE	_____	_____
COST OF CHARTER BUS	_____	_____

PASSPORT REQUIRED □ YES □ NO   PROOF OF CITIZENSHIP _____

LAUNDRY SERVICE □ ONE DAY OTHER _____

BABY SITTERS □ YES □ NO CONTRACT _____COST _____

ARE PETS ALLOWED □ YES □ NO

ARE KENNELS AVAILABLE NEARBY □ YES □ NO _____ COST

LIQUOR ANY SPECIAL RULES _____

*ATTACH LIQUOR PRICE LIST

BROCHURES YES □ NO □ COST _____

POST CARDS □ YES □ NO COST _____

OTHER PROMOTION AIDS _____

NOTES: _____

Rooms

	CLASS			TOTAL	RATES		
	1	2	3		FAP	MAP	EP
SINGLE	____	____	____	____	____	____	____
DOUBLE	____	____	____	____	____	____	____
TWIN	____	____	____	____	____	____	____
STUDIO	____	____	____	____	____	____	____
PARLOR	____	____	____	____	____	____	____
JR. SUITE	____	____	____	____	____	____	____
EX. SUITE	____	____	____	____	____	____	____
CABANA	____	____	____	____	____	____	____

TOTAL NUMBER OF ROOMS AVAILABLE FOR CONVENTION _____

RUN OF THE HOUSE RATE SINGLE OCC.   ____ ____ ____

                 DOUBLE OCC.   ____ ____ ____

CHILD IN ROOM COST _____

THE ABOVE RATES ARE: ☐ NET ☐ GROSS ☐ COMMISSIONABLE

                                    ☐ NON-COMMISSIONABLE

TAX _____% OTHER CHARGES _____

CHECK IN TIME   _____

CHECK OUT TIME _____

COMPLIMENTARY ACCOMMODATIONS _____

COMPLIMENTARY SERVICES _____

NUMBER OF DAYS BEFORE AND AFTER THAT CONVENTION RATE APPLIES _____

_____

RADIO IN ALL ROOMS	☐ YES	☐ NO
TELEVISION IN ALL ROOMS	☐ YES	☐ NO
	☐ COLOR	☐ BLACK & WHITE
TUB & SHOWER IN ALL ROOMS	☐ YES	☐ NO

EXPLAIN DIFFERENCES IN:

                 LOCATION   _____

                 FURNISHINGS   _____

                 OTHER   _____

Dining Rooms

| | | MAP |
| | | FAP OR |
NAME	HOURS	CAPACITY	A LA CARTE
_____	_____to_____	_____	_____
_____	_____to_____	_____	_____
_____	_____to_____	_____	_____
_____	_____to_____	_____	_____
_____	_____to_____	_____	_____

MEALS SERVED

| | | | | LIQUOR |
NAME	BREAKFAST	LUNCH	DINNER	SERVICE
_____	☐	☐	☐	☐
_____	☐	☐	☐	☐
_____	☐	☐	☐	☐
_____	☐	☐	☐	☐
_____	☐	☐	☐	☐

MEALS   FAP OR MAP FOOD PORTION OF RATE

          BREAKFAST _____

          LUNCH   _____

          DINNER   _____

SURCHARGES _____

SPECIAL PRINTED MENU ☐ YES ☐ NO _____ COST (ATTACH SAMPLES)

BUFFET BREAKFAST AVAILABLE ☐ YES ☐ NO

CONTINENTAL BREAKFAST AVAILABLE ☐ YES ☐ NO

VARIETY OF SELECTION EACH DAY ☐ YES ☐ NO

KOSHER FOOD AVAILABLE ☐ YES ☐ NO

SPECIAL OUTOOR MEALS _____

GUEST CHARGES _____ ROOM SERVICE CHARGES _____

COFFEE BREAK CHARGES _____ WITH PASTRY _____ WITHOUT PASTRY

COCKTAIL PARTY CHARGES _____ PER DRINK _____ PER PERSON PER HOUR

FINAL GUARANTEE TIME FOR FOOD FUNCTIONS _____

ATTACH WINE LIST _____

NOTES: _____

Gratuities

			AMOUNT
BLANKET	_____ YES	_____ NO	_____
SPECIAL LIST	_____ YES	_____ NO	_____
BELLMEN	_____ YES	_____ NO	_____
WAITERS	_____ YES	_____ NO	_____
MAIDS	_____ YES	_____ NO	_____
RECEPTIONS	_____ YES	_____ NO	_____
FOOD	_____ YES	_____ NO	_____
FOOD	_____ YES	_____ NO	_____
BEVERAGE	_____ YES	_____ NO	_____

CHARGE TO _____ INDIVIDUAL _____ MASTER ACCOUNT

Accounting

_____ YES _____ NO   MASTER ACCOUNT

_____ YES _____ NO   SINGLE FOLIO

_____ YES _____ NO   TWO FOLIO

_____ YES _____ NO   SPEEDY CHECK OUT AVAILABLE

_____ YES _____ NO   CREDIT CARDS ALLOWED (LIST BELOW)

_____

_____

_____

_____

_____

_____ YES _____ NO   PERSONAL CHECK ALLOWED

_____ YES _____ NO   MAY GUEST SIGN BILL AND HAVE IT FORWARDED FOR
                     PAYMENT

Insurance

HOTEL COVERAGE FOR THEFT AND INJURY _____

Union

ANY LABOR CONDITIONS TO BE AWARE OF _____

Registration

☐ INDIVIDUAL
☐ CONTROLLED BY CONVENTION PLANNER
☐ LIST REQUIRED _____ DAYS IN ADVANCE OF MEETING
LOCATION OF REGISTRATION DESK _____
GUESTS ARE ☐ PRE REGISTERED ☐ REGISTER ON ARRIVAL
CONVENTION BUREAU PERSONNEL AVAILABLE TO STAFF REGISTRATION DESK
☐ YES ☐ NO

Meeting Rooms

FLOOR PLANS AVAILABLE ☐ YES ☐ NO, PLEASE ATTACH.
ANY CHARGES ☐ YES ☐ NO, IF SO, EXPLAIN _____

NAME	SIZE	THET.	SCRM	RECP.	BANQ.	SOUND	LIGHT	A.C.	STAGE

TYPE OF ROOM DIVIDERS _____
NEARBY WORKROOM LOCATION _____ SIZE _____
EXHIBIT AREA AVAILABLE _____
NOTES: _____
_____
_____

Staff

TELEPHONE NUMBER

OWNER _____

GENERAL MANAGER _____

SALES MANAGER _____

CONVENTION MANAGER _____

RESERVATION MANAGER _____

CATERING MANAGER _____

BEVERAGE MANAGER _____

MAITRE D'HOTEL _____

CHEF _____

DINING ROOM CAPTAINS _____

ROOM SERVICE MANAGER _____

BELL CAPTAINS _____

TRANSPORTATION MANAGER _____

HEAD HOUSEMAN _____

BAGGAGE MAN _____

ELECTRICIAN _____

SECURITY OFFICER _____

SOUND MAN _____

SET-UP MAN—MEETING ROOMS _____

HOUSEKEEPER _____

FLORIST _____

PHOTOGRAPHER _____

SOCIAL DIRECTOR _____

HOUSE PHYSICIAN _____

PUBLIC RELATIONS _____

AUDITOR _____

CASHIER _____

GOLF STARTER _____

TENNIS PRO _____

NIGHT AUDITOR _____

NIGHT MANAGER _____

NOTE: ADVISE ANY CHANGES IMMEDIATELY

Equipment

STANDING LECTERNS _____ LIGHTED □ YES □ NO
TABLE LECTERNS _____ LIGHTED □ YES □ NO

	NUMBER	SIZE	TYPE
TABLES	_____	_____	_____
CHAIRS	_____	_____	_____
EASELS	_____	_____	_____
BLACKBOARDS	_____	_____	_____
BULLETIN BOARDS	_____	_____	_____
FLIP CHARTS	_____	_____	_____
POINTERS	_____	_____	_____
PLATFORMS	_____	_____	_____
PROJECTORS	_____	_____	_____
MICROPHONES	_____	_____	_____
SCREENS	_____	_____	_____
PIANO	_____	_____	_____
FLAGS	_____	_____	_____
GAVEL	_____	_____	_____
LIGHTING	_____	_____	_____
STAGE	_____	_____	_____

SOUND SYSTEM □ LOW IMPEDENCE □ HIGH IMPEDENCE
ANY UNION OPERATORS REQUIRED □ YES □ NO _____ COST
IS EMERGENCY OXYGEN AVAILABLE □ YES □ NO
NOTES: _____
_____

Shipping

BEST METHOD _____ AIR _____ TRAIN _____ TRUCK
BEST CARRIER _____
TIME ALLOWANCE _____
CUSTOM REQUIREMENTS _____
STORAGE FACILITIES _____
PROPER WAY OF ADDRESSING SHIPMENTS _____
_____
_____
_____

Special Features

SHOPPING TOURS _____

SIGHTSEEING TOURS _____

RESTAURANTS _____

ENTERTAINMENT _____

HISTORICAL SITES _____

HOTEL SPECIALTIES _____

LOCAL ATTRACTIONS _____

Churches

DISTANCE

BAPTIST   _____

CATHOLIC   _____

EPISCOPAL   _____

JEWISH   _____

LUTHERAN   _____

METHODIST   _____

PRESBYTERIAN   _____

OTHER   _____

                 _____

                 _____

                 _____

                 _____

Recreation

GOLF _____ YES _____ NO, LOCATION _____ DISTANCE _____

NUMBER OF HOLES _____

TOURNAMENT PLAY AVAILABLE	_____ YES	_____ NO	
BLOCKS OF STARTING TIMES AVAILABLE	_____ YES	_____ NO	
GREENS FEES	_____ YES	_____ NO	_____ COST
CARTS	_____ YES	_____ NO	_____ COST
CADDIES	_____ YES	_____ NO	_____ COST
CLUB RENTAL	_____ YES	_____ NO	_____ COST

NUMBER OF SETS AVAILABLE _____

BAG STORAGE	_____ YES	_____ NO	_____ COST
PUTTING GREEN	_____ YES	_____ NO	
LUNCH AT CLUBHOUSE	_____ YES	_____ NO	
FAP	_____ YES	_____ NO	
BAR AT CLUBHOUSE	_____ YES	_____ NO	
TRANSPORTATION	_____ YES	_____ NO	_____ COST

SWIMMING _____ YES _____ NO, LOCATION _____ COST _____

CABANAS	_____ YES	_____ NO	_____ COST
INSTRUCTION	_____ YES	_____ NO	_____ COST
SCUBA EQUIPMENT	_____ YES	_____ NO	_____ COST
CHAISE LOUNGES	_____ YES	_____ NO	_____ COST

FISHING _____ YES _____ NO, LOCATION _____

BOAT RENTAL	_____ YES	_____ NO	_____ COST
TACKLE	_____ YES	_____ NO	_____ COST
TRANSPORTATION	_____ YES	_____ NO	_____ COST
LICENSE REQUIRED	_____ YES	_____ NO	_____ COST

TENNIS _____ YES _____ NO, LOCATION _____ COST _____

NUMBER OF COURTS _____

LIGHTED	_____ YES	_____ NO	
TOURNAMENT PLAY AVAILABLE	_____ YES	_____ NO	
RACKET RENTALS	_____ YES	_____ NO	_____ COST

SKATING _____ YES _____ NO, LOCATION _____

SKATE RENTALS	_____ YES	_____ NO	_____ COST

HORSEBACK RIDING _____ YES _____ NO, LOCATION _____

GUIDE REQUIRED	_____ YES	_____ NO	_____ COST
SKEET	_____ YES	_____ NO	_____ COST
ARCHERY	_____ YES	_____ NO	_____ COST
VOLLEYBALL	_____ YES	_____ NO	_____ COST
BASKETBALL	_____ YES	_____ NO	_____ COST
LAWN BOWLING	_____ YES	_____ NO	_____ COST
BOWLING	_____ YES	_____ NO	_____ COST
PING PONG	_____ YES	_____ NO	_____ COST
SHUFFLE BOARD	_____ YES	_____ NO	_____ COST
MOVIES	_____ YES	_____ NO	_____ COST

OTHER _____

OTHER _____

MEETING PLAN

The Meeting Plan is made up of "daily schedule sheets" and various other function sheets arranged in proper sequence. Start with the daily schedule sheet for the first day and list on it each function at the proper time with its location and number of people involved. For each function listed fill in the appropriate sheet and place these in the book in proper order following the daily schedule sheet. Repeat this process for each succeeding day; then number each page from front to back and enter the proper page numbers on the daily schedule sheets. This provides a complete detailed layout of the entire meeting with all necessary information in chronological order.

Meeting

LOCATION _____

NUMBER OF PEOPLE_____   TYPE OF SEATING _____

STAGE _____   LIGHTING _____

MICROPHONES _____   TAPE RECORDER _____

PROJECTOR _____   SCREEN _____

LECTERN _____   FLAG _____

STAGE PROPS _____   PIANO _____

ASH TRAYS _____   PADS AND PENCILS _____

ICE WATER _____   AIR CONDITIONING _____

PHOTOGRAPHER _____   PROJECTIONIST _____

REST ROOMS _____   ENGINEER _____

NEARBY NOISE _____   STOP MUZAK _____

STOP TELEPHONE _____   AWARDS _____

INSTALL TELEPHONE _____   SET UP MAN _____

BOWL AND TICKETS FOR DOOR PRIZES _____

COFFEE BREAK _____

ADDITIONAL REQUIREMENTS _____

_____

_____

_____

_____

_____

_____

_____

ROOM LAYOUT: (USE BACK OF SHEET IF NECESSARY)

Plan

COMPANY NAME _____

ADDRESS _____

GROUP NAME _____

IN CHARGE _____

DATES_____

NUMBER OF ROOMS _____   NUMBER OF SUITES _____

    ARRIVAL PATTERN   _____

                         _____

                         _____

    DEPARTURE PATTERN   _____

                         _____

                         _____

                         _____

SPECIAL ROOMING REQUIREMENTS

                         _____

                         _____

                         _____

CABANAS _____

RATES _____

COMPLIMENTARY ACCOMMODATIONS   _____

                                      _____

DEADLINE FOR ROOMING LIST _____

ACCOUNTS GUARANTEED BY COMPANY _____ YES _____ NO

ACCOUNTING — SEE STANDARD PROCEDURE

PERSONAL CHECKS GUARANTEED BY COMPANY UP TO _____

GRATUITIES _____

                         _____

                         _____

Daily Schedule Sheet

COMPANY NAME _____

DATE _____

TIME	FUNCTION	LOCATION	NO. PEOPLE	PAGE NO.
A.M. 7:				
8:				
9:				
10:				
11:				
12:				
P.M. 1:				
2:				
3:				
4:				
5:				
6:				
7:				
8:				
9:				
10:				

Seminars

COMPANY OFFICIAL IN CHARGE _____

HOTEL OFFICIAL IN CHARGE _____

DATE _____   TIME _____

NUMBER OF PEOPLE _____

LOCATION

1. _____	8. _____
2. _____	9. _____
3. _____	10. _____
4. _____	11. _____
5. _____	12. _____
6. _____	13. _____
7._____	14. _____

OF PEOPLE PER ROOM _____   STAGE _____

TYPE OF ROOM ARRANGEMENT _____

LIGHTING _____   MICROPHONES_____

TAPE RECORDER _____   PROJECTOR _____

LECTERN _____   SCREEN _____

STAGE PROPS _____

ASH TRAYS _____   PADS AND PENCILS _____

ICE WATER _____   AIR CONDITIONING _____

PHOTOGRAPHER _____   PROJECTIONIST _____

NEARBY NOISE _____   ENGINEER _____

REST ROOMS _____   STOP MUZAK _____

STOP TELEPHONE _____   SIGNS _____

INSTALL TELEPHONE _____   SET UP MAN _____

COFFEE BREAK _____

ADDITIONAL REQUIREMENTS _____

ROOM LAYOUT: (USE BACK OF SHEET IF NECESSARY)

Special Event

COMPANY OFFICIAL IN CHARGE _____

HOTEL OFFICIAL IN CHARGE _____

DATE _____   TIME _____

NUMBER OF PEOPLE _____

LOCATION _____

DETAILS _____

_____

_____

_____

_____

_____

_____

_____

_____

_____

_____

_____

_____

_____

_____

_____

_____

_____

_____

_____

_____

_____

Meal

COMPANY OFFICIAL IN CHARGE _____

HOTEL OFFICIAL IN CHARGE _____

DATE _____ TIME _____

TIME OF FINAL GUARANTEE _____

_____ BREAKFAST _____ LUNCH _____ DINNER

LOCATION _____

NUMBER OF PEOPLE _____ TYPE OF SEATING _____

MENU _____

_____

COST _____ LIQUOR SERVICE _____

WINE _____ CHAMPAGNE _____

STAGE _____ DECORATIONS _____

CENTERPIECES _____ NUMBER OF TABLES _____

LECTERN _____ MICROPHONES _____

TABLE NUMBERS _____ HEAD TABLE _____

LIGHTING _____ DANCE FLOOR _____

AWARD TABLES _____ AIR CONDITIONING _____

MUSIC _____ ENTERTAINMENT _____

PHOTOGRAPHER _____ ENGINEER _____

REST ROOMS _____

ADDITIONAL REQUIREMENTS _____

ROOM LAYOUT: (USE BACK OF SHEET IF NECESSARY)

Reception

COMPANY OFFICIAL IN CHARGE _____

HOTEL OFFICIAL IN CHARGE _____

DATE _____ TIME _____

LOCATION _____ ALTERNATE_____

OF PEOPLE _____ # OF HORS D'OEUVRES TABLES _____

OF BARS _____ # OF BARTENDERS _____

BRANDS OF LIQUOR

_____ _____

_____ _____

_____ _____

_____ _____

_____ _____

COST _____ PER DRINK _____ PER PERSON

HORS D'OEUVRES

_____ _____

_____ _____

_____ _____

COST AND NUMBER _____ PER ORDER _____ PER PERSON

DECORATIONS _____

FLOWERS _____ MUSIC _____

ADDITIONAL REQUIREMENTS _____

ROOM LAYOUT: (USE BACK OF SHEET IF NECESSARY)

Registration

COMPANY OFFICIAL IN CHARGE _____

HOTEL OFFICIAL IN CHARGE _____

DATE _____ TIME _____

LOCATION _____

NUMBER OF TABLES _____ CHAIRS _____

SIGNS _____ BOXES/ENVELOPES _____

TYPEWRITER _____ TELEPHONE _____

POST CARDS _____ ACTIVITY CARDS _____

BLACKBOARD _____ BULLETIN BOARD _____

SHOWCASE/PRIZES _____ BOX/GOLF SCORE CARDS _____

LOCAL LITERATURE _____

SPECIAL LIGHTING _____

ADDITIONAL REQUIREMENTS _____

_____

_____

_____

_____

_____

_____

_____

_____

_____